MAHMOUD DARWISH

Journal of an Ordinary Grief

♆

Translated from the Arabic
and with a foreword by Ibrahim Muhawi

archipelago books

Library of Congress Cataloging-in-Publication Data
Darwish, Mahmud.
[Yawmiyat al-huzn al-'adi. English]
Journal of an ordinary grief / by Mahmoud Darwish ; translated [from the Arabic]
by Ibrahim Muhawi. – 1st ed.
p. cm.
First published as Yawmiyat al-huzn al-'adi in 1973.
ISBN 978-0-9826246-4-7
1. Jewish-Arab relations. 2. Darwish, Mahmud.
I. Muhawi, Ibrahim, 1937– II. Title.
DS119.7.D2913 2010
305.892'74–dc22   2010027211

Archipelago Books
232 Third St. #A111
Brooklyn, NY 11215
www.archipelagobooks.org

Distributed by Consortium Book Sales and Distribution
www.cbsd.com

Printed in the U.S.A.

Cover art: Henri Michaux, *La Cordilléra des Los Andés*

Jacket design by David Bullen

This publication was made possible by the generous support of
Lannan Foundation, The National Endowment for the Arts,
and the New York State Council on the Arts, a state agency.

Manufactured at Thomson-Shore, Inc., in Dexter, Michigan
Visit Thomson-Shore on the web at www.thomsonshore.com

This translation is dedicated
to the people of Gaza

Acknowledgments

I am grateful to Lannan Foundation for the grant of a residency that helped get this project on its way. In particular I wish to thank Patrick Lannan, president; Martha Jessup, program director (Residency Program); Douglas Humble, residency manager in Marfa (Texas); and Ray Freese, assistant residency manager. I would also like to take this opportunity to express my appreciation of the Foundation's commitment to cultural freedom. A number of individuals have also contributed to the welfare of this book: Afaf Ackall kindly volunteered her own copy of the 2007 edition of the work. Muhammad Siddiq was generous with advice on meaning and language on the numerous occasions when I asked for it. Jill Schoolman, founder of Archipelago Books, has been supportive throughout. With her careful editing she has done readers of this translation a favor. Thanks also to Dan Avnon and Leonard Schwartz, who provided helpful information on Martin Buber. It also gives me great pleasure to acknowledge the contribution of Jane Muhawi, my partner in this work, whose enthusiasm I treasure and whose literacy, mastery of the sound patterns of English, and editorial skill always leave her stamp on my work.

Foreword

Journal of an Ordinary Grief (*Yawmiyyât al-Huzn al-'Âdî*, 1973) is the first of three major prose works that form a trilogy spanning Darwish's career. (We always have to be careful in selecting descriptive terms for Darwish. True, these are prose works, but they are far from being "prosaic.") The second, *Dhâkira lil-Nisyân* – a memoir of the 1982 Israeli invasion of Lebanon – appeared in 1985, and my translation (*Memory for Forgetfulness*, University of California Press) in 1995. The third volume, *Fî Hadrat al-Ghiyâb* (*In the Presence of Absence*), appeared in 2006, two years before the poet's death. To the extent that they are based on the poet's actual experience, these works may be considered autobiographical, though *Journal* tends more in that direction than the other two.

In this book we read about the poet's experience of house arrest, his encounters with Israeli interrogators, and the periods he spent in prison. Readers should not expect straightforward autobiographical narrative, however, but a work in the symbolist mode, in which the semantic range of words is extended. From the beginning of his career, Darwish had already adopted Palestine as his cause célèbre, but it is in this work that he makes an explicit declaration of his mission: "Your cause and your life are one. And before all this – and beyond it – it is your identity." This identification is part of the symbolist equation of himself and Palestine. It is as much a poetic identification as it is political; in other words, it is an equation of the poetic with the political. To avoid confusion, readers should keep this identification in mind. Expressions like "your death," "the first death," or "the nineteenth anniversary of your killing," do not refer to his personal death but to the loss of Palestine in 1948. The pronoun *I*, for example, can refer to the poet as an individual but can also stand for the Palestinian people as a whole. The author uses a number of forms here, principally dialogues with imaginary partners. The opening part of the book is a dialogue that places the reader in a strange space because we cannot tell who is talking to whom until the end of the section, when we discover that the dialogue has been between the author and himself as a child. In *Journal*, as in all of Darwish, we are placed in the middle of an encounter between writing and history where writing gives shape to the homeland.

This work first appeared in Beirut (Dâr al-'Awda), two years after the poet left his homeland to become an exile. In taking a close look at the existentially complex situation of the Palestinians in Israel proper, and in exploring the meaning of resistance and the ambiguity of his identity as an Israeli Palestinian – an ambiguity that becomes a major theme and poetic figure in all his work – this prophetic book provides the background for the poet's decision to become an exile. Irony is probably the literary mode most appropriate to exile. Loss of homeland and life under occupation – the major themes of this work – are not ordinary griefs. Darwish's irony, which undoubtedly stems from the complexity of being an Israeli Palestinian, is a distinguishing feature of all his work.

In preparing this translation I faced a difficult decision. The opening parts of the work as it originally appeared in 1973 were omitted in later editions (Riad El-Rayyes Books). The scholar in me decided that the 1973 edition must be translated in full because it forms part of the record of Darwish's corpus – aside of course from the significance of its content. After careful consideration I decided to include the omitted material as an appendix, except for Darwish's own introduction to the original edition ("These Pages"), which I put at the beginning for the thought it articulates about writing and the homeland. Particular attention, however, should be paid to the opening section of the appendix, which explains the dilemma Darwish faced in living in Israel but without citizenship: "The ground of perplexity lay between the truth of your being and your current legal status."

I was guided in the process of translation by two precepts from Darwish himself: rhythm and the sentence as a unit of meaning. The first section of his 2005 volume of poems, *Don't Apologize for What You've Done*, consisting of 47 poems, is called "The Passion for Rhythm" (literally, "lusting after rhythm"), and the first poem of that section is called "The Rhythm Chooses Me." ("The rhythm chooses me / It chokes on me.") This is the most explicit and powerful articulation of Darwish's concern with rhythm, which always was a major esthetic preoccupation for him.

Toward the end of *Journal*, Darwish refers the reader to the Arabic sentence ("Going to the Arabic Sentence on May 15"). This phrase is an excellent illustration of the symbolist mode mentioned earlier: in combing together words or phrases that apparently do not belong side by side, the poet extends the metaphorical potential of the individual words as well as the meaning. The verb "go" – itself rich in connotation – makes of language a place, thereby extending the sense of the word *sentence*, which, in addition to its literal reference to the sentence, can in this context also refer to the Arabic language, including its grammar and sound system; to the political rhetoric of the Arab regimes; to Arabic prose; and (beyond the boundary of language) to the Arab peoples and their countries.[1]

None of these, however, is as troubling as the literal reference to Arabic sentences, because this is the domain that lies within the power of the translator. Darwish, the accomplished poet, is also an acknowledged master of Arabic prose – that is, of the Arabic sentence. After all he himself is writing Arabic sentences and that obviously is what the translator must consider as the basic unit of translation because the sentence establishes the rhythm of his prose. Yet in a quotable line in one of his later poems, Darwish says, "Neither is prose, prose; nor is poetry, poetry." Such an outlook does not lead to the production of easy sentences. Darwish's prose often shares the complexity and obscurity of his poetry, reflecting the complexity he felt in his identity.

The sentence being the basic unit of rhythm in Darwish, in rendering *Journal* into English I used his sentences, regardless how complex, as the basic units of translation. Insofar as it has been possible to do so, I have maintained the rhythm of his syntax throughout, translating sentence for sentence. Yet though one can make an effort at the macro level of rhythm to maintain the integrity of the sentence, it nevertheless remains true that each language has its own sense of rhythm within the sentence. Arabic moves from right to left, and its words are constructed differently from the way English manages its vocabulary. In translating within the sentence, I have relied on my ear to create sound harmonies and a consistent rhythm, but without sacrificing meaning.

Darwish does not provide sources for his citations, assuming that readers will be familiar with the context of his statements. While this consideration may have been true for some Arab readers in 1973, we cannot assume it to be the case for the reader of this translation. Because the issues Darwish raises in this work – in the body of the text as well as in the appendix – are even more urgent today, I have provided endnotes to supply context and specific reference to sources that I was able to locate. Where possible I have used existing English translations of the material he quotes.

These Pages

This book does not attempt to compose the life history of a generation of Palestinians who forged their language in facing the long occupation. It is only a small voice carving a shape in the rocks of Galilee, which have become a prison cell and a horizon, though the gateway to the world has now opened out to other wars and other places of exile. From the start, writing has shaped the other form of the homeland, not asking what lies beyond. The voice radiates out to borders that do not end and realizes that what lies outside is a vacuum. Palestine, which flows out of itself and our blood, which urges us to recast it with all the tools of the impossible, liberates us and holds us prisoner without giving us a way out. Do the boundaries of the earth begin and end with our blood?

The battles do not end, and the language remains on edge. These pages do not tell the whole story. They only set down the beginnings of a small voice that shook the rock a little. The homeland is distant and near, and in this everyday grief and everyday death the writing gets written, or tries to get written, so that this ordinary grief may stop accepting being acceptable.

MAHMOUD DARWISH

Journal of an

Ordinary Grief

❧

The Moon Did Not Fall into the Well

❧

—What are you doing, father?

—I'm searching for my heart, which fell away that night.

—Do you think you'll find it here?

—Where else am I going to find it? I bend to the ground and pick it up piece by piece just as the women of the fellahin pick up olives in October, one olive at a time.

—But you're picking up pebbles!

—Doing that is a good exercise for memory and perception. Who knows? Maybe these pebbles are petrified pieces of my heart. And even if they're not, I would still have gotten used to the effort of searching on my own for something that made me feel lost when it was lost. The mere act of searching is proof that I refuse to get lost in my loss. The other side of this effort is the proof that I am in fact lost as long as I have not found what I have lost.

—What else are you doing, father?

—When I chance upon pebbles that look like my heart, I transform them with my fingers on fire into words that put me in touch with the distant homeland. We then become a language that can turn into flesh.

—Is there something else you want to say?

—I do, but I don't understand the words, for the woman I'm talking to turns into another exile.

—When you were young, were you afraid of the moon?

—That's what they say. But it's not true that children are always afraid of the moon.

If it weren't for the moon, I would've become an orphan before my time. It hadn't yet fallen into the well. It was higher than my forehead and closer than the mulberry tree in the middle of my grandfather's yard. The dog used to bark when the full moon rose. When the first shots rang out, I was surprised that a wedding celebration should be taking place that evening. And when they led me away to join the long caravan, the moon was our companion on a road that later I understood was the road of exile. And if it weren't for the moon – as I just said – I would've been separated from my father.

—What else do you remember?

—I remember I learned to travel on my own at an early age. My mother had gone to Acre, and I was angry because she had left me behind. How I loved Acre! It was the most remote place in the world years ago. And now – what a paradox! – it has become the most remote again. I carried my five years and walked in the asphalt street in the direction of Acre.

—Did you know the way?

—The paved road that went west meant only one thing: a trip to Acre. It was very hot, and I cried from the heat and thirst. Many times I sat down to rest, and thought of heading back but was ashamed to admit defeat.

—What did defeat mean to you?

—To seek, and not find. To start, and not finish. So I continued to Acre. I stopped near a crossroads at the entrance to the city. It did not occur to me to continue in the same direction. I went south instead, and it led me to a sand dune overlooking the sea. Mother wasn't there. So I went back to the crossroads and headed north. That way led to Beirut, and I knew Mother wasn't there. I went back to the crossroads again and headed west into the heart of the city. I went into a shop and asked for water. They asked me what I was looking for, and I said, "I'm looking for my mother."

—How does a village boy look for his mother in a crowded city?

—As I did. I was sure I would spot her among the thousands of faces. And if it weren't for my fear of the approaching evening, I wouldn't have gone back to the village without her, but a child of five must sometimes face defeat. I returned to the crossroads and headed back empty-handed. I was afraid of night approaching from the sea, and waited by the side of the road. A truck driver stopped and asked where I was going. I said, "Al-Birwa."

My mother was already in the house, but the rest of the family and the neighbors were out searching for me in all the wells of the village. When children got lost, it was assumed they had fallen into wells. My mother cried, and I cried with her. And when she had recovered from her joy, she gave me a beating. My grandfather then came and took me away, and gave me some sweets. That was the end of my first journey.

It was my first taste of Acre. I have always searched there for something I couldn't find. I looked for my mother but she had already returned to the village. Some years later, I searched for my sweetheart but she was getting married to another man. I searched for work but poverty was my lot. And I searched for my people but found a prison cell and a rude officer. Acre was the last border to the world, and the beginning of effort and failure. Its wall was eroding with time.

—Do you remember anything else about the beginning of the world?

—I remember an obscure shape that assisted me in calling for help from imagination and dream. Reality was subject to a process of interruption before it could achieve its budding form in my awareness. Later circumstances made it necessary for me to go back to the dream to safeguard my existence, for it completed what was missing. And that has left me in a dream that must always be justified by necessity, and not by flying on the wings of exuberant imagination. The earth thus takes the form of a bird and a rock at the same time. For the situation in its current state – even if it is not legitimate – cannot become a part of you without being tied to the dream, which then turns more solid than a rooted tree. And the dream in its general state – even if it is not luxuriant — will no longer serve as an incentive without being tied to a rock, no matter how the shape of this rock changes. True, things would not be so precious unless their condition served as a touchstone of your existence – unless they become an occasion for conflict. But if you were deprived of them, their value would not be the measure of your life, regardless of their price. Otherwise, how are we to explain why the poor, when forced out of their country, persist in facing death to return to a poverty they had left behind? There is something we forget in the rush to memorize the ringing slogans of the revolution: human dignity. My country is not always right, yet I cannot exercise genuine rights except in my homeland.

—Why are you avoiding me? Are you trying to put a distance between yourself and the past?

—To make it clear to you that I do not defend a past happiness, exactly as I do not celebrate a past misery. Perhaps it is due only to our high opinion of it that our homeland is justice and beauty. Yet it did not become so beautiful merely from projection caused by deprivation. It is a dream in its actuality, and an actuality in its dream. We do not long for a wasteland, but for a paradise. We long to practice our humanity in a place of our own.

—Take this further.

—The lives of thousands of victims and martyrs are now gone. They were not deceived. Some of them never saw the homeland, and died from the virus of love. Yet the map is not always wrong; neither is history. Why has there been such a consensus among prophets, conquerors, and the poor to be in love with history to the point of killing? The erotic dance that the Mediterranean Sea performs with the waist of Mount Carmel ends in the birth of the Sea of Galilee. And there is a sea they call the "Dead Sea" because something must die in this paradise, so that life will not be boring. Further, to counter the crowding of the Upper Galilee with forests, Jerusalem had to prove that rocks possess the power of living language. This is my homeland. My father's friend, who lived in Beirut, was not exaggerating when he said he could smell the lemon trees in Jaffa when they blossomed in season. Then he died.

—Is it the lost paradise then?

—Beware of this expression, because to believe it would be to surrender to a state of being that has reached its legal and existential limits. The difference between a lost paradise in its absolute sense and the lost paradise in its Palestinian meaning is that the former understanding would keep the condition of longing, and psychological and rightful belonging, out of the sphere of the conflict. As long as the struggle continues, the paradise is not lost but remains occupied and subject to being regained. I'm not basing my thought here on the notion of "losing the battle but not losing the war," which rests upon justifying oneself in facing up to the lost battle. But I do mean that Palestinians cannot look at their homeland from the perspective of the lost paradise, as the Arabs look back on Andalusia or as the faithful look forward to their reward in Paradise. Between Palestine and Andalusia there is a difference that resembles death. Some well-intentioned tourists in the revolution, taking as their point of departure only the beauty of form and the control of solidarity, see a similarity that can lead only to bad consequences. They will cry even more than you if you accept this similarity, placing your rights under siege and your existence behind a wall of inspired longing. But when longing resorts to the gun as an expression of the distance between Palestine and Andalusia, you will find that these tourists, who adore the lamentations of ancient peoples, will protest because the beauty of historical symmetry has been violated. The idea of the lost paradise is tempting to those who are not possessed by a pressing question, but inflicts upon the Palestinian condition an accumulation of tears and weakness in the blood. This is how my homeland surpasses Paradise: it is like Paradise, but it is also attainable.

—Didn't you stand at this edge one day when you were no longer a child?

—Not so fast! The mere fact of birth does not lay claim to a place. The place in which you are born is not always your homeland, unless your birth takes place in the natural course of events within a historical community. If the birth is not part of a natural community, the place of birth is accidental. What a difference between the birth of Mahmoud and that of Yisrael, which both occurred in the same place! That conquerors should reproduce themselves in another people's land does not guarantee for them the right to call it a homeland. But when a people reproduce naturally in their homeland – *that* is the continuity of the nation and the source of its legitimacy. The fact that forced exile has made it impossible for this continuity to emerge does not bring about a decisive change in the order of things. What I'm saying is that the equation does not emerge unless it comes about as a result of the marriage of a people to their rightful land. The hostile birth taking place now is the result of a relationship between conquerors, a sword, and the Torah. Therefore, we do not fear the dictates of justice in this matter.

The meaning of all this is that I did not simply find myself outside the realm of childhood. My departure was not voluntary. It was not a journey, but expulsion and exile. The circumstances of my life had come to an abrupt end but remained alive in my awareness. The confrontation in that exile with extremely harsh conditions that could not be negated or resisted on their own terms but only by returning to my roots helped me not to feel the loss of my childhood so intensely. We are more mature now, and can object to the practice of laying the blame for Palestinian misery solely on the condition of exile itself. That would be a victory for exile and for those who brought it about, and would allow the criminal to sow the seeds of discord between the wounded and the hospital administration. I do not say this to praise the administration or the soundness of its management, but to remind us that the conquerors must never be far from our awareness when we indulge in internal squabbles.

You weren't able to hold back your anger in exile when your classmates reminded you that you were Palestinian and had no right to excel. Those insults were the first clues to an awareness that would take hold of you in a few years, when you realized that your situation was not simply a matter of asking for equal rights, or a question of getting hold of more bread in a crisis. Even at that early age you sensed instinctively that your deliverance from these insults consisted in getting rid of the circumstances that brought them about. And that was the beginning of your necessary (not accidental) link with your first world. It was then that your vaguely remembered village, with its narrow alleys, sitting on a hill in the Plain of Acre was transformed into the solution to a problem you had not yet grasped. As a result the childhood things that you had left behind, and your return to reclaim them, became the means by which you could prove you were not different from the others: these were evidence that you did once possess the accessories of life, and need not be subject to insults. Your awareness of this evidence was particularly keen on holidays. The other children put on new clothes and spoke about feasts. And you stood alone with your father in a line of beggars to obtain clothing and a portion of food that came from anonymous sources.

—When did that happen?

—In 1949, after the exodus.

—And why didn't it take place in 1948, the year of the exodus?

—Ah! We were tourists then. My grandfather carried a big bag full of money, and it was like a picnic in Lebanon. He took us to the apple orchards so we could pick choice fruit from the trees. And every week he took us to Beirut, which was the first city I ever saw after Acre. It wasn't a flight; it was like a picnic. We were waiting for the Arab armies to defeat the conquerors in a few weeks, and we would then go back to al-Birwa. We didn't live in a refugee camp. We passed through Rmeish, then spent one night in Bint Jbeil, which was a tumultuous human pen teeming with the loud cries of exiles. That was the second night we spent away from home. The first we spent at a Bedouin camp, where scores of "guests" ate fried eggs from a single dish. In Jezzine – where we stayed a while – I saw the water running in canals right through the houses, and I saw the waterfall. When it got very cold there we moved to Damur, where we wandered in the banana orchards, played on the shore, and swam in the sea. One day I crossed a wide street ahead of my brother, who followed and was hit by a car. There were no wounds, but he was in shock for a number of years before he snapped out of it. Grandfather was a good reader and read the newspapers, which assured us of a quick return. We sat around him in a circle as he read in a powerful voice, his eyeglasses nearly falling off. The newspaper took him from readiness to pack his bags, to a state of not hurrying, and from there to waiting, until we noticed a weakness beginning to creep into his voice, which became more subdued as his glasses started to move back up. On winter nights the brothers in exile and conversation would exchange opinions about the battles taking place in the land of Palestine, until it was announced that al-Birwa had fallen.

—Had it not fallen before?

—It was occupied for one night, then liberated by villagers with primitive weapons and help from neighboring villages. As soon as it was liberated they made ready to gather the harvest waiting for them on the threshing grounds, but the Arab Army of Salvation took it over, and we don't know how the Jews got it after that.

Twenty years later after many Arab cities had fallen, the thoughts I was sharing in Hebrew with a friend at a restaurant did not please a man sitting there, and he set to defending Israeli oppression with what he considered an irrefutable argument. He said you don't know these Arabs, and if you knew them, you wouldn't speak about justice in this manner. I asked him to tell me more. He knit his brow and said, "Have you heard of a village called al-Birwa?" "No," I answered. "Where is it?" "You won't find it on this earth," he said. "We blew it up, raked the stones out of its earth, then plowed it until it disappeared under the trees."[2] "To cover up the crime?" I asked. He corrected me, protesting, "No, it was to cover up *its* crime, that damned place." "And what was its crime?" I asked. "It resisted us," he answered. "They fought back, costing us many casualties, and we had to occupy it twice. The first time we were eating dinner, and the tea was hot. The villagers surprised us and took it back. How could we accept such an insult? You don't know the Arabs, and now I'm telling you." I told him I was Arab, and that it was my village. He apologized politely but awkwardly, talked of peace, then invited me to his shop, where he was auctioning off furnishings and household utensils plundered from the city of Quneitra.

A few days later two Jewish settlements celebrated the silver jubilee of their establishment on the lands of al-Birwa. I was speaking at a press conference that day and talked about the oppression of the Arab community, but a correspondent for a newspaper called *Settlements* interrupted me, and I mentioned the news of the celebration. He apologized politely but awkwardly, and talked of peace.

This is the way they are. They commit the crime, deny it, and when the victim confronts them they sidestep the question by talking of peace.

"I gave you a land on which you had not labored, and cities which you had not built, and you have lived in them; you are eating of vineyards and olive groves which you did not plant."[3]

—Did you happen to visit al-Birwa after that?

—When Grandfather realized that our presence in Lebanon was not going to be just a vacation or a picnic and the war had ended with the loss of everything, when he realized that the fruits in the orchards he had planted, now being eaten by the Jews, had turned into a card for receiving food relief, he became aware that our departure had been a mistake. He saw that his absence from the land was now exile, and set about replacing hopes invested in [Arab] armies with the need to regain his belonging to the land through his actual presence on it.

The shock created by defeat due to dependence on weapons carried by others, with justice as one's sole weapon, ushered in the awareness of "stealing back" into the occupied land – no matter the consequence or the price – to establish your presence and leave the insults behind. Under threat of death we stole back at night over rocky terrain. We didn't travel together in case the caravan of returnees ran into danger on the way. After two nights of an exhausting crawl on rough ground we all met up in a village. There we were now, back in Palestine! We didn't know we were going to be exchanging refugee status in Lebanon for refugee status at home. And we didn't realize that our physical presence in the homeland constituted an absence in the eyes of the law the conquerors quickly implemented. They called us "present-absentees" so we would have no legal right to anything. At the same time we found out that thousands of these returnees were shoved into trucks as soon they were arrested and immediately dumped on the border like damaged merchandise. We knew that hundreds were shot dead so that others would stop thinking of returning. We also knew that my aunt's husband, who tried to steal in from Lebanon, had not yet arrived. Which was more painful, to be a refugee in someone else's country or a refugee in your own? When, as a result of the current state of affairs, the Arab citizen sees the Israeli plow biting into his land and his body to produce grain and grapes for those who have come from all parts of the world, and he cannot do anything about it and is even forbidden to make a pilgrimage to it – the question that mental anguish constantly imposes is, "Can the land be so holy?" For the Palestinians, the answer is yes.

Villages were closed off by a set of military regulations whose violation would cost you a prison sentence and a fine. Scores of villages were destroyed because of their fertile land, or as punishment for their resistance to the sword emerging from the Torah. Their inhabitants were forbidden to go near them, no matter what changes may have occurred in the security fence of Israel. Because of this, it was impossible to visit our village. We realized that our return was not going to be the answer to the question of our living standard, or the solution to our alienation, but was only an alternative to voluntary exile. It was an attempt to get closer to the source of our rights and our identity, to make us more intensely aware of being there in person. Here is my identity, and yet how alienated I feel! My alienation here is a positive thing because its causes are beyond my control, and because I am present in person. The torment that charges my relationship to the hallowed and forbidden earth is thereby transformed into a potential for rejection. On the road from Deir el-Asad to Acre stands al-Birwa still on the same rise. I did not find it by means of the government list that gave it another name. What led me to it was the huge carob tree where, many years ago, I started the search for my mother and the pieces of my heart that were saturated with rain and longing.

A place is not only a geographical area; it's also a state of mind. And trees are not just trees; they are the ribs of childhood. The tears also flowed freely from the tips of my fingers as the bus passed quickly by. Upon our return, the sadness of my childhood came back. This dream standing before me, why didn't I just wrap it around myself even once so I could say I have felt the joy that kills? The soldiers were guarding the dream, but I will enter it when they sleep.

—Did they sleep? And did you enter?

—That happened later. Tears were no longer appropriate for someone my age, and I was testing my ability to face the child I had left behind when I was seven years old. The thornbushes were now taller than me, and we were both lost, the child and I. We didn't know which of us would run into the other first. I had never before seen birds with such colors of blue and green. I was gashed by a sharp thorn, and felt happy because I had arrived. I was deep into the feeling of being on a pilgrimage, but didn't find a Kaaba. What gives the land all this wildness except desertion? The cactus hedge into which the British had thrown my father, burying him in its limbs after they had hacked them with pickaxes, had grown back now. The doctor had to remove a hundred thorns from his skin, in addition to the ones buried deep in his flesh. Whose luck was better, Father? That of the one who swallowed the spines and continued cultivating the land, or the one who came to the land and found nothing but thorns? A young shepherd there was surprised when I greeted him. "Where are you from?" From Yemen? I told him this was my village, and he thought I was a Roman because he thought these were Roman ruins.

"If we move into a region where there are wild animals to which the Jews are not accustomed – big snakes, etc. – I shall use the natives, prior to giving them employment in transit countries, for the extermination of these animals. [And I will give big rewards to those who bring in the skin and eggs of these snakes.]" This is what Herzl said, and maybe this shepherd who came from Yemen thought I was searching for snakes.[4]

I continued on the path of stones and longing, searching for the boy I had left here. I didn't find the mulberry tree he climbed or the courtyard where he used to lose himself. Nothing! Nothing – except the shell of a church without a bell. I went inside, and the cows drew me along idly. I was no longer ready to be content with ruins as an embodiment of the dream, because my feeling of belonging was no longer instinctive. It became more mature, and the content of the dream, not its eruption, became my cause.

—You didn't tell me why you left? Why didn't you reach these conclusions before all this loss?

—My father said they didn't fully grasp what was happening. It was going to be a quick battle with guaranteed results, they had imagined. The departure from the villages was a way of saving the body from death, with no corresponding awareness of what leaving the land meant. The idea of the homeland, it seemed, did not need intellectual effort, mobilization of the community, or planning. The home, the orchard, and the plow were not weapons. And the call to stay put – it seems – was not part of the battle because the forces required to put it into effect had not been organized and the consequences of not doing so had not been foreseen.

—Does this mean the fellahin had no patriotism?

—No. The proof is that they volunteered to join the fight on their own from purely national motives, but the organization was poor. The prevailing impression – or ruse if you wish – was that the exit would be temporary, for a few days only. So, why should children, women, and old people die for nothing if the departure was going to be temporary, with victory and return guaranteed? The Israelis used the exit as an excuse to claim we had no attachment to our homeland and were therefore not worthy of one if we could so easily leave it behind. But they deceive only themselves when they believe their own claims, for they supplemented the prevailing rumor that the exit was temporary with guns and daggers that gave the Arabs a strong incentive to leave. They offered them the following option: either death or departure for a few days. Emptying Palestine of its Arab inhabitants was not an emergency measure imposed by circumstances, but part of an ongoing Zionist strategy before the establishment of the state, during the [1948] War, and after. They carried out this strategy violently with their weapons, and justified it on religious grounds from the example of Joshua Son of Nun and the text "The Day of the Lord is a day of terror."[5] And they justified it on secular grounds from their own practices. It was Menachem Begin who said, "If it weren't for Deir Yassin, there would be no state of Israel." They proclaimed the aim of the Deir Yassin Massacre from loudspeakers mounted on cars that went around blaring out, "Leave, or suffer the fate of Deir Yassin." And in all the villages they occupied afterward they gathered the inhabitants in the main square and made them stand in the sun for several hours. Then they chose the handsomest young men and shot them dead in front of the other villagers in order to force them to leave, in order to let news of the massacre spread to villages not yet occupied, and to purge their repressed historical resentment.[6] They also found legal justification in the claim that the Arabs sold their land. Sadly, it is possible to find certain Arab groups that have believed this Israeli lie while making no effort to learn that until 1948 the Jews owned no more than six percent of the total land of Palestine.

—And you, what did you do with your land?

—Ask rather what the land did. It vanquished my grandfather, who died waiting. It gave my father gray hair from hard labor and misery, and it gave me an awareness of injustice before my time. My grandfather was a prosperous landowner. After what happened, he became a "present-absentee" and spent his days at the office of the military governor waiting for a permit to travel to Acre for no other reason than to get a glimpse of his land from the window of the bus. He spent his days reading newspapers and his nights mulling over the past. And waiting. He's the one who brought me up, and I loved him more than my father, who spent his days in toil, extracting bread from stone quarries. Grandfather taught me reading, the borders of the land, and the ages of the olive trees. He brought me books from Acre and took me with him to his friends to show off the child who could memorize the old poetry and read without making mistakes except in the Sura of Yasin. I read to them from the historical romances of Antar and the Zir and from the novels of Jurji Zaydan until I fell asleep. In the morning I went to school, where they refused to enroll me officially because my father's name was not on any government list. He who left for Lebanon and returned in a year or two is not a citizen, but he who came from Warsaw after two thousand years does have rights and a homeland.

Late one night a police captain struck the door of our adobe brick house with his truncheon. He woke up the family – grandfather, grandmother, my parents, and four children – all crowded into a single room that served as sitting room, bedroom, and kitchen. The captain directed a question at my grandfather, "Did your children return from Lebanon?" Grandfather confessed to the "crime," and the captain hauled the father and uncle away under arrest on the charge of stealing back into their own country.

Grandfather did not stop living on hope, so he moved to another village closer to his land. One summer he got around the law by leasing from a Jewish merchant the seasonal crop of watermelons produced on his land. Thus the owner of the land had an opportunity to buy what his land produced. Grandfather had little experience with commerce and lost money on the deal, but he did gain an opportunity to spend many hours in his old field. One day, in the sun, he explained to me the history of this land that one could not distinguish in any way from his skin. Grandfather's attachment to the national identity embodied in his ownership of the land and his longing to bring back his connection to it – severed by law but still joined emotionally and historically – were more powerful than the unexpected misery he suffered from having been deprived of it. If his sense of identity were only a question of livelihood, he could have solved the problem by cutting the connection that stood in his path to freedom from hardship. He preferred living in hardship to selling his land, which became the foundation of his dignity but was no longer a source of livelihood as it had been.

After it was confiscated, the land became a source of misery, as well as the foundation of personal and national dignity. Having opted for dignity, he died within sight of the scene of the crime and his torture: "I will not sell them my land, even if I die of hunger." He left this understanding of the land as an inheritance for my father, who had a much harder time of it. He earned a living for eight people residing in a mud-brick house not fit for a pampered animal. Toiling in the stone quarries to earn a living for a large family that needed food, clothing, medicine, and books was nothing more than a slow suicide. He woke up at five in the morning and returned at five in the evening to go to sleep so that he could wake the next morning and carry on his daily ordeal. The quarry was far away in an area that they called "Military Maneuvers," and getting there meant having to sign a death document, according to which the bearer gave up the right to his life and donated it to the state of Israel in case of death. Friends urged him to sell the land to lighten his unbearable burden, but he always refused: "I won't sell, even if I die in that quarry."

He always said that hard labor was not shameful, but a black conscience was. I was in my last year of elementary school when I recited my first poem in front of a large audience brought together under the auspices of the military governor to celebrate the establishment of Israel. I said some words against the government and its victory, and against oppression and colonization. The village elder was livid. "This boy is going to bring ruin upon us," he said, "after he's brought endless trouble to his parents and family." "Why don't people heed the rules of hospitality?" he asked, and said other things we hear these days. The military governor, whose name was Dov, called me in the next day. He scolded me, and struck me, but I didn't cry. Then he said he would prevent my father from working in the quarry by revoking his death permit, and I cried on the way home because that meant I would feel greater cold and hunger, and would not be able to transfer to the secondary school. School costs were exorbitant, for education was not free, as some people believed. At home my father was supportive, and said, "God will provide."

The water at the village spring was scant, and we had no money to lease a well. Refugees are cursed in their homeland and out. Nobody gave us water for free except the sky in winter. My mother spent her days waiting at the stingy spring for the trickle of water to fill the jar. She was beautiful and severe, terrorizing everyone in the house. When she was by herself she sang continually on every possible occasion. She calmed my sister with melancholy songs about hard luck and longing for lost things. Songs that were like primitive psalms. She never went to a wedding celebration, but always went to funerals in our village and neighboring villages. She could never feel happy, but had a great capacity for shedding tears, and her gift for irony was brilliant.

My uncle put Herzl's promise into practice, for he worked as a laborer in the settlement set up on his and his father's land. He worked in construction, renovation, agriculture, and other kinds of hard labor "to which the Jews are not accustomed," but he didn't earn any rewards because he never brought in any snake skins or eggs. He would sometimes take a bunch of grapes from the vine that he had planted, now become Jewish property, and bring them home to offer to his family, one grape at a time.

Thus, acting from natural inclination and self-respect, they all chose long years of hardship over the tiny comfort that could be gained from giving up their right to a piece of land, land whose loss would have deprived them of their world and which in any case did not belong to them or their enemies but to future generations, because in the unfolding of the world and time this choice kept justice on their side.

—And what have you inherited from them?

—The same meanings, but the perspective has changed. Their waiting was negative, for to them the land meant the specifics of earth, orchards, and ownership that protected their dignity and livelihood. But for my generation it means – in addition to these – a field of struggle and a future. Longing is a human energy that stays passive. It's a negative weapon. The struggle has gradually been taking different forms. First came rejection of the status quo and faith in the individual's ability to bring about change. Then came collective resistance against the forces and conditions that made us citizens without a country, a resistance that does not put itself under siege in memories but sets them free for building a better future in the things that we do every day. Belonging to the land, and the homeland, brings no result unless it means becoming part of the forces joined in the struggle. That's what we realized early on.

—Was that possible?

—Within the limited number of choices available to us then.

—Where did hope come from?

—From the outside, always from the outside. Prisoners can resist within the means available to them. But the complete destruction of the prison cannot come about except through the window. The window was bigger at the beginning because our Arab brothers were closer to us.

—Where does your grief come from?

—From the pores of my skin.

—And where does your happiness come from?

—From the crying of children being born into a hellish life, and from the boots of fighters heading for Paradise.

—Do you remember when we parted?

—When grandfather died and was not buried in the place of his choice, and the newscast expressed no shame.

—Why do you always turn to the world?

—I don't turn to the world. Rather it is the world that comes and puts me under siege.

—When shall we meet again?

—When you tap on the wall of my chest and jump out to sit facing me as you usually do. But I beg you to keep your visits to a minimum.

—Are you going to kill me?

—When a person kills his childhood he commits suicide. And I have need of you as witness to a generation. Don't come back often, for ugliness fills the cities, and many of my friends are dying these days.

—Don't forget me!

He went back into my breast to climb the mulberry tree in the courtyard of the old house and catch the moon that did not fall into the well.

The Homeland:
Between Memory and History

℘

I

What Is Homeland?

The map is not the answer. And the birth certificate is no longer the same. No one has had to face this question as you have, from this moment till you die, or repent, or become a traitor. To be content is not enough because contentment does not bring about change or blow anything up, and the wasteland is immense. The desert is not always bigger than a prison cell. So, what is a homeland? It is not a question you can answer and then go on your way. Your cause and your life are one. And before all this – and beyond it – it is your identity. It would be the simplest thing to say, my homeland is where I was born. But when you returned, you found nothing. What does that mean? It would be the simplest thing to say, my homeland is where I will die. But you could die anywhere, or on the border between two places. What does that mean? After a while the question will become harder. Why did you leave? Why did you leave? For twenty years you have been asking, why did they leave? Leaving is not a negation of the homeland, but it does turn the problem into a question. Do not write a history now. When you do that, you leave the past behind, and what is required is to call the past to account. Do not write a history except that of your wounds. Do not write a history except that of your exile. You are here – here, where you were born. And where longing will lead you to death. So, what is a homeland? You are part of a whole, and the whole is absent and subject to annihilation. And why are you now afraid of saying "homeland is where my ancestors lived"? You reject the pretext of your enemies, for that is what they say.

—What did you learn in school?

—*Salute the bird returning from the distant land to my window in exile. O bird, tell me, how are my ancestors and my people?*

—And the song that came before that?

—They erased it.

—What are the words of the song they erased?

> *Salaam to you*
> *Land of my ancestors*
> *In you it's good to dwell*
> *And for you it's good to sing.*

There is not a huge difference between the two songs, except the difference in a longing that comes from afar, and a longing that rises from nearby. Both songs declare love for the same land, and both define homeland in terms of ancestry. The first is by a poet who lived in Russia, and the second is by a poet who lived in Palestine and never saw exile or heard of it. In a short period of time the first song overcame the second, and the second poet started to sing his longing for the distant homeland. The youth who remained in the homeland were forbidden to sing the song of their poet. Their path to a future was hostage to their mastery of the songs of the Jewish poet who lived in Russia. The Arab teacher who dared teach a song expressing love for the homeland lost his job, accused of anti-Semitism and incitement against the state of Israel. Then we grew up a little, and they taught us the difficult epics of the Jewish poet, but from al-Mutanabbi we took only this:

> *The enmity is in you, and*
> *You are the enemy*
> *And you are the judge.*

They are the enemy and they are the judges.
And they are the ones who define "What is homeland?" for us. They say:

You will run from Egypt with Moses, and strike the sea with your staff. The sea will part and the tribes of Israel will pass. The sea will then devour their enemies. You will stay in the Sinai desert for forty years. You will make peace with the Lord, and then return.

And they are the ones who define "What is homeland?" for us:

Herzl sat and thought about the fate of his persecuted people. He came up with the idea of Zionism as the only path to the only secure salvation. The Jews will not realize themselves and they will not be able to bring into being the historic mission of Jewish renaissance except by a return to the homeland of their ancestors . . . to Palestine.

And when you ask the teacher about the fate of the Palestinian Arab people and their country, he whispers in your ear to stop taking risks by daring to question the sacredness of history. But when the teacher is Jewish, he will explain to you what Chaim Weizmann said at the Paris Peace Conference in 1919: "The Land of Israel must be as Jewish as England is English." And when you insist on asking about the fate of the Palestinian Arabs, he will reassure you that Weizmann added, "The Zionists will not come into Palestine as conquerors. They will not force anyone to leave."

They won't force anyone to leave?

II

Do not ask the history teacher. He earns his livelihood by telling lies, and as the history becomes more remote the lies become more innocent and less harmful. This history teacher knows you very well. At a distance of five minutes from the school is the beginning of the Acre Road heading east to Safad. As soon as you leave Acre you come to a small forest of olive trees in the middle of which there is a small hill that overlooks a flat, green plain. On this hill not long ago you were born. Your childhood is still close to everything – the hill, the plain, the blacktop road, and the first gunshots. If it were not for the moon that night, they might have lost you forever, as happened with a mother from Haifa when there was no moon. The guns attacked her home, and she grabbed something she thought was her baby and rushed into the nearest boat in terror. While on the sea to Acre she discovered that the baby was only a pillow, and from that day she lost her mind. How many infants became pillows? And how many pillows were taken for infants? So, what is a homeland? The homeland of a mother is her child, and the homeland of a child is the mother. "The Arabs sold their land and left" – so say our friends and our enemies. Apparently, death is not martyrdom when it does not demand a price. And Deir Yassin was not Arab propaganda as some now claim. To ask an unarmed population to die does not constitute a correct understanding of the meaning of homeland. And those who now say the Arabs sold their homeland and left had earlier claimed that staying in the homeland was treason. For them war is a picnic, and flight a journey.

That night you did not understand anything. You asked your father but he forbade you from asking because you were too young. They left you in a neighboring village and went away. The history teacher said they did not drive anyone out. In southern Lebanon you became a refugee, receiving your rations from the United Nations Relief and Works Agency. And you waited for the return. In southern Lebanon you understood what homeland was for the first time. It was that thing which had been lost. It was this expected return. And when you returned after a year or two to that thing which was lost, you discovered that you yourself were lost.

—Don't let anyone know you were in Lebanon.

—Where was I then?

—In the Bedouin encampments in northern Palestine.

In a short while Palestine will be forbidden. Its name will be Israel, the Israel that Moses carried after he parted the sea with his staff.

—And what if I do say I came from Lebanon?

—Since you stole back in, and the world has changed, you won't be able to get an identity card. Every week there is a funeral in the village. They keep stumbling upon the corpses of those slipping back in, whom wilderness, cold, or bullets had wiped out. The history teacher is still telling you that they did not drive anyone out. And when you ask, "How could Israel be as Jewish as England is English if they didn't drive anyone out?" he forbids you to ask the question and says, "History is history, and politics is politics."

At a distance of five minutes from this village there is a road that leads from Acre to Safad. As far as you are concerned this is not a road but a boundary that separates the land where you are an exile and a refugee from the land that is your homeland. On the south side of the street is the land of your father and grandfather, now cultivated by settlers from Yemen. The moment they reached your land they defined their destiny and that of their children. At the same time they decided your fate. The moment they became citizens you became a refugee. If your feet should touch this land – your land – you will be taken to court, and from there into exile outside the country. And when you question them, sometimes they accuse you of treason and other times of imagining things. At this point you grasp for the second time what homeland means. It means longing for death in order to bring back your land and your birthright. Homeland is not only land; it is land and birthright combined. Justice is on your side, but the land is in their hands. After they took the land by force they started speaking of acquired rights. Their "right" was historical and consisted of memories, and now it is land and military power. Without power, you have lost history, land, and rights.

III

> Just you listen to me . . . Immigrants of ours will come to this Khirbet what's-its-name, you hear me, and they'll take this land and work it and it'll be beautiful here . . . We'd open a cooperative store, establish a school and maybe even a synagogue. There would be political parties here. They'd debate all sorts of things. They would plow fields, and sow, and reap, and do great things. Long live the Hebrew Khizeh! Who, then, would imagine that once there had been some Khirbet Khizeh that we emptied out and took for ourselves? We came, we shot, we burned; we blew up, we expelled, drove out, and sent into exile.[7]

These are not the words of an Arab. This is a rare cry of conscience by an Israeli writer more than twenty years ago, which accurately defines the idea of the homeland. It is an answer to history and to the history teacher. *This* is the basis of the Israeli "homeland" – not rights, or history, or escape from persecution. Only violence: "We drove them out and took their land. We set the village on fire, blew it up, and sent the people into exile." But this cry is rarely heard in the clamor of propaganda and lies. And when you follow with them the path of logic to its end, they will confess, but they wind up the discussion with this unchanging answer: "There was no choice." They are waiting for time to transform aggression into a right that will become accepted in due course.

Khirbet Khizeh was not the only place. All of Palestine was translated in this manner. The houses Israelis live in are inhabited by ghosts. Yet their preoccupation with proving they are worthy of a homeland and with repelling all that hinders their sense of identity renders them deaf and releases them from the responsibility of questioning the horror of the method used to form that identity. With the passage of time, the image of the Arab person would shrink and melt away. It was a burden on the conscience, then became part of the natural décor, then settled into the image of an enemy who must be destroyed and who has no right to a homeland, absolutely no right.

During the June War [of 1967] many Israeli soldiers were surprised to find that Arabs have a memory, and remember a homeland that was lost. What surprised them most was that the children born after the loss of the country were still attached to it. An Israeli soldier related that when he went into one of the refugee camps he discovered that the people lived there exactly as they had previously lived in their villages. They were organized as they had been before: the village was the same and the street was the same. That soldier was shaken. Why?

—I could not comprehend this. Nineteen years have passed, and they are still saying, "We are from Bir al-Sabi'."

A soldier who was a poet told me that never in his entire life did he feel he was an alien in Palestine until he went into one of the villages in the West Bank after the last [1967] war. He was in military uniform, and saw a young girl in the street who looked at him in a way that shook the ground under him. From a look he could not explain in the eyes of a child, he realized he was an occupier. He did not hide his surprise at the rejection he saw in the eyes of that child. Where did her memory come from? And who taught her that she had a homeland? Who taught her?

Is it a struggle between two memories?

Jewish memory is one of the basic components of the claim to a right in Palestine. Yet it is incapable of admitting that others also possess the sense of memory. Israelis refuse to live side by side with Arab memory. They refuse to admit the existence of this memory, even though one of their mottos is, "We will not forget." One of the basic topics in Israeli education, a primary topic in the order of Zionist priorities, is to keep general awareness permanently focused on memory as a way of mobilizing nationalist sentiment. They have always said, "May I forget my right hand if I forget you, O Jerusalem!" After the holocaust to which European Jews were subjected at the hands of the Nazis, their basic motto became: "We will not forget, and we will not forgive." Every year the Israelis remember their dead, and life comes to a stop. There are museums, forums of instruction, and special programs all dedicated to remind new generations of the Holocaust. Amos Elon devotes a whole chapter to this subject in *The Israelis*, where he says that commemoration of the Holocaust proves to new generations one of the basic tenets of classical Zionism, that "without a country of their own the Jews will remain the dregs of humanity and prey to evil animals."[8] The book makes clear that Israeli policy uses the Holocaust as a form of emotional blackmail.

Israeli culture insists on saturating the memory of citizens with the holocaust in Europe in order to intensify their feelings of isolation and alienation from the rest of the world. These feelings constitute a basic part of Israeli temperament and subjectivity. As a result, the nurture of Israeli memory is dedicated to a single political goal: to keep reminding the people that they are always subject to annihilation, and that returning to the "Land of Israel" and remaining in it are the only political and historical guarantees of security – in addition to furthering the Zionist claim to Palestine.[9]

It is the duty of not only the Jew to remember the Nazi massacres. All people whose conscience is still alive and all friends of freedom share the memory of the victims of Nazism and take heed, especially when we see a historical resemblance between Nazism and racist movements in the world today. No matter the degree of enmity between Arabs and Israelis, no Arab has the right to feel that his enemy's enemy is his friend, because Nazism is the enemy of all peoples. That is one thing.

But Israeli excess in taking out their hatred on another people is something else, because one crime cannot redeem another. That Palestinians and other Arabs should be asked to pay the price for crimes they did not commit cannot possibly serve as an indemnity for the disaster. Israelis pride themselves on having been the vanguard as exiles and refugees throughout history, to the point where they have turned this into a privilege and a distinguishing characteristic. Yet they who possess exile and refuge as one of their senses have become totally incapable of realizing that other people also possess this sense. It would not be an exaggeration to say that Israeli Zionist behavior toward the original inhabitants of Palestine is similar to the practices applied by the Nazis against the Jews themselves. It would also not be an exaggeration to say that the behavior of Israel and the Zionist movement vis-à-vis the rest of the world gives one the impression that they are using the blood of the victims as a commodity. They utilize the money and equipment they receive as payment for the victims of Nazism to destroy another people. Consequently, it would again not be an exaggeration to say that the methods Israel uses to commemorate the victims of Nazism may be characterized as forms of blackmail, given that the basic aim behind saturating the Israeli people with the consciousness of catastrophe is to saturate them at the same time with feelings of vengeance, not on their killers but on another people – the Palestinian people, who are themselves victims. Unsophisticated Zionists are not ashamed to boast of the fact that the loss of six million people – assuming the number is correct – gave them a homeland.[10]

IV

They acknowledge no right for you, and they do not credit you with a memory.

You go to the police station at four in the afternoon to declare that you exist. Your friend says, "Join me in an adventure. Taking possession of beauty is the real adventure." To the south of Haifa, on the road running parallel to the sea, you light your cigarette and don't put it out except in your open wound. The car swerves to the north a little, and you find yourself inside a treasure. The sign at the entrance says, "This is 'Ayn Hûd." The real name of the village is 'Ayn Hod, but the Arabic letter Dod is impossible to transliterate. Down with the homeland, but not with one letter of the language! And what is 'Ayn Hod? In a valley from which rise three knolls where the road leads to the sea, you see Arab houses that look from the outside as their owners had left them. Every house is hidden from the rest of the world in a little forest. The original inhabitants were moved to the top of one of the knolls that looks over their open wound in the valley. Why this sadism? They can see their homes with their new inhabitants and their neglected lands but they are not allowed to visit the grasses and the stones. Beyond this, the state does not grant them the right to a memory.

My friend has a friend who is an artist living in this village. He was set on keeping the old Arab house in its original state. "Lovely décor that reminds me of the Orient," thus said this painter, who recounted the story of his escape from Nazism. We asked him about the land on which he lived now, and he said he loved it. We reminded him that the mere fact of his need for Arab décor to establish a connection to the Orient nullified the authenticity of his relationship to the land, giving him the character of a tourist. He said, "I have no other choice." Then he pointed out the similarity between the Palestinian Arabs and the Jews. The condition of being refugees brings them together, and now each helps in shaping the other. We said that what also brings them together is the focus of the conflict between them. In saving yourself from being a displaced refugee, you forced the other side to the point in the circle from which you started. Seen this way the equation no longer holds. When you find yourself canceling me out of my being, and when I insist on keeping it, the relationship between you and me becomes one of conflict. Not because I object to your being or to the possibility of a shared existence, but because I object to the negation of my being that arises from the way you carry on with yours.

In situations like this the discussion never ends because the acknowledgment of truth is a negation. Only a few steps away the original inhabitants of the village sit and watch. And it is not an Arab sort of Zionism – as some claim – that the Palestinian Arab should cling to his memory for two decades. The very proposition of a Zionist memory as an entitlement is sign of an Israeli weakness more than it is a justification, for the appeal to memory nullifies Israeli astonishment that the Palestinians are holding on to memories still fresh. He who allows himself a flood of tears for two thousand years cannot blame the one who has been crying for twenty years of having merely fallen prey to delusion. Besides, holding a monopoly on tears – if we can put it that way – is not a national trait that calls for pride. On May fifteenth – at a specified hour in the morning – the sirens are sounded in all parts of Israel as a call to mourn those who fell in the "War of Independence." Pedestrians are nailed to the spot, wherever they may be. Vehicles come to a halt. Labor and machinery stop as a declaration of a mourning that precedes joy and celebration. And what does the Arab do? Cry from within, or burst from the pressure. The declaration of the birth of Israel is at the same time the declaration of the death of Palestine. This moment, then, is the historical rupture that separates two states of being. But you are forbidden to remember or to call upon your memory. The assault on this memory, then, has become a Zionist goal and a national demand of the first order. No. It is not Arab Zionism to remember the assassination of your homeland. At this rupture/paradox in history the tears of the opposites converge. You cry over a lost homeland, and they cry over those who were lost in search of a "homeland" just born.

You stand still in a street that devours you, just as you in turn devour your rage and defeat. What is homeland? To hold on to your memory – that is homeland. They suffer great sadness. All their holidays are sad. But it is the sadness of distant memories that renders current happiness the size of the universe. At night they dance, embracing life with abandon. Why do you demand that they understand you? You always said, "Let me write just one essay in their defense, and then I can die." It does not seem that Arab oil is going to grant you this wicked wish. The sadness of victors is deceit and hypocrisy, and it does not indicate progress but inferiority. They have borne the griefs of history and released them in you, and it is demanded that you feel no sadness. You are forbidden to feel sad, O Palestinian Arab. They commemorate whores and stones and heroes of aggression, and they commemorate their true victims, but you are forbidden to commemorate anyone or anything. More than that: they call upon you to celebrate their victories over you, and if you refuse you will be punished. They did not permit you to commemorate the victims of Kufr Qasem. It is a fact that their victims – all their victims – fell at the hands of others. And your victims – all your victims – fell at their hands. When the day to commemorate the Kufr Qasem massacre arrives, they surround the village and the cemetery, and forbid anyone to enter, because sadness is forbidden to you. Even more than that: they confiscate more land in the Galilee. They translate the Galilee yet again with a new Jewish city, Karmiel. The inhabitants of three Arab villages whose lands were confiscated hold a demonstration, and they are put under siege and arrested – and Karmiel comes out the victor. They choose the day to celebrate its establishment so as to coincide with Kufr Qasem Day itself, not only as provocation and scorn, but also to make it clear they have the power to keep you down. These are refugees that bring an end to the state of being refugees by creating other refugees. So, my friend the painter, what does your statement that similarity in refugee status brings us together mean? It means nothing – nothing except robbery. The refugees scattered by Nazism found a homeland for themselves in Palestine, and the refugees driven out by Zionism, where are they to live? Where?

V

That child, delivered by his mother's womb to the earth, delivered by the police into exile, and whom longing had brought back to a predatory land, did not realize that a philosophy of things was demanded of him: he did not realize that the measure of being worthy of belonging to the land, or belonging to it without being worthy of it, depended on mental gymnastics. Why should your ability to answer the question, "What is your country?" be proof of the authenticity of your belonging to this country? The true homeland is that which cannot be known or proved. As for the country that emerges from a chemical formula or from a theory in an institute, it is not a homeland. Your awareness of the need for proof of the history of a rock and your ability to manufacture proof does not give you priority of belonging vis-à-vis someone who can tell when the rains will come from the smell of that rock. For you that rock is an intellectual exercise, but for its owner it is a roof and a wall. And a rock is not a rock when it can change into a totem that you carry in your bag and bring out as a demonstration in your lectures. The rock is a rock when it can be your neighbor, O friend looking for a totem that may serve as an identity. And what else will you say to me? That this country was a desert! Don't go that far in your lies. Palestine was never a desert. You have no right to take me to task concerning my worthiness, for I am not a lawyer for gardens and sand. You did not come to defend the right of sand to water, or the right of trees to greenness. If my country was like that, it would not have tempted you to occupy me, burn me, and expel me. And to this day, we have not yet arrived at the stage of facing the chalk circle because we have not come to judgment. And who is to be the judge?[11] You! How could you be enemy and judge at once, unless you were my lover, and yet my relationship to you is not one of love? Your claim used to be blood and kinship, and now you claim worthiness to win the case at the chalk circle court. You draw the circle when you wish, and erase it as you see fit. You do not recognize my existence, and you nullify my link to this country, claiming it to be nothing more than a passing courtship and will disappear in time. And how did you prove this? By violence and force alone. This is the way of the world. The justifications of the powerful carry more weight – always. By force alone you defined the shape of your link to my homeland, and the shape of my relationship to this link.

> The Arabs exist in Palestine in a relationship of "I-It." The Jews, on the other hand, exist in Palestine in a relationship of "I-Thou."

This is the voice of the existential philosopher Martin Buber. He says that human beings are connected with what is around them in one of two ways – "I-It" or "I-Thou." The "I-It" relationship exists in place and time and is subject to causality. In this relationship, there is no freedom, only necessity. The "I-Thou" relationship, on the other hand, exists outside space and time, beyond causality. Here there is freedom, and not necessity. On this understanding, human existence is inauthentic if it is an "I-It" relationship. The Jewish faith is the only religion based on the "I-Thou" relationship. And because the Jews still believe in the truth of this religion, they are the chosen people, and on that basis the state of Israel must come into being in Palestine. The relationship of the Jews to Palestine is not the same as that of the Arab relationship to it, because Arabs exist in Palestine in an "I-It" relationship, and for that reason it is easy for them to sever that relationship, and it would be possible to transfer them elsewhere.[12]

When it comes to life on the ground, however, another writer – one more in touch with the facts – ruptures the freedom of the relationship that connects Jews to Palestine, giving rise to a rare case of feelings of guilt. Ideology may appear clean to its proponents as long as it remains abstract, but when it is put into practice it takes the shape of a crime. In a story that caused a great stir, A. B. Yehoshua portrays the collapse of the "innocence" of Zionist ideology against the actuality of the crime committed against another people. Zionist critics accused him of terrorism, of advocating national suicide and masochistic congruence with the enemy. The events of the story take place in a Jewish National Fund forest planted over the ruins of an Arab village and funded by a group of Jews who live outside Israel. The hero of the story is an unnamed Israeli student who is searching for solitude in order to do research on the Crusades. An elderly, idealistic official in charge of the forests suggests that he take a job as a fire lookout. The student takes his books and papers and sets out for the isolated wood, with nothing that links him to the outside world except a pair of binoculars and a telephone connected to the fire station. It was not by accident that the writer should choose as a setting for the story a Jewish National Fund forest growing over the ruins of an Arab village, for this forest is a symbol of the realization of the Zionist dream, and the village stands for the tragedy of the Palestinian Arab people that came out of the realization of the Zionist dream. It is also not by chance that the subject of the research is the Crusades, given the resemblance they suggest between past and present.

The Israeli student is not alone in the forest or wood. There is also an Arab fellah whose tongue was cut out in the [1948] war ("It's us or them; this doesn't change anything"). The Arab has remained in the ruins of his village working as a laborer in the wood, and there is a young girl with him. The three of them live in the forest without any tension at first, but the tension mounts in time as the action unfolds. With cypress trees in the background and signs that bear the names of revered contributors ("Louis Schwartz of Chicago," "The King of Burundi"), the student feels that the ceremonious promenade of official delegations, tourists, and other visitors coming and going resembles a caravan of Crusaders. One of the visitors says, "Where exactly is this Arab village that is marked on the map? It ought to be somewhere around here, an abandoned Arab village." "A village? No, there is no village here," the fire watcher replies. "The map must be wrong, the surveyor's hand must have shaken." [13]

At first the student spends his days and nights searching for signs of fire in the wood. He tests the alarm system, and watches the movements of the Arab, suspecting that he is preparing for revenge. Then it becomes gradually clear that the student wants a fire to break out in the wood. He tries to do it himself with the kerosene the Arab brings for that purpose, but the attempt fails. From that point their relationship becomes very strong. The student tells the old man about the history of the Crusades, and the mute Arab emits animal-like sounds, answering with hand gestures. "He wishes to say that this is his house and that there used to be a village here as well and that they have simply hidden it all, buried it in the big forest."

When the Arab does start the fire in the forest, the student lights up with enthusiasm and happiness, and takes part in the operation. He does not call for help. Someone else sounds the alarm, but it is already too late. At dawn the hero strolls over the remains of the fire, and very gradually a small Arab village emerges from the fog and the smoke: "There out of the smoke and haze, the ruined village appears before his eyes; born anew in its basic outlines as an abstract drawing." Amos Elon explains: It is clear that the forest symbolizes the Israeli society that has arisen over the ruins of another society.[14] Yehoshua said in a newspaper interview that his story is not ideological but describes the actual situation in the country, where something was erected over the ruins of something else. There is a feeling of guilt.

There are other examples in modern Israeli writing where feelings of guilt are revealed about the creation of Israel and the conflict between Israelis and Palestinians over the one "homeland." But it is a guilt arising from self-confidence, one of the sorts of confession made by the powerful at a time of ease when the force of victory is mixed with a little pinch of liberalism and humanity, when it is too late and the massacre has already taken place, but it is never, under any circumstances, an expression of contrition or regret. It resembles to a great extent the internal dialogue of a murderer after the crime. Some American writers, for example, do portray the tragedy of Native Americans, expressing sympathy with them.

A certain Israeli writer finds puzzling the absence on the Arab side of the phenomenon of guilt and self-recrimination. This puzzlement, the proof of a desire to treat victim and killer as equals, demands that the victim cry together with his killer over a shared misery – the misery of the victor who gained a homeland but was forced to act like an oppressor, and the misery of the vanquished who lost a homeland and asks his oppressor to treat him with fairness. In what way can a Palestinian call himself to account, and how can he harbor feelings of guilt? Undoubtedly he does have such feelings – but only in relation to himself and to his homeland, not to the one who defeated him – and occupied his country and his psyche.

Do not ask, after this, what homeland means.

The map does not constitute an answer because it is very much like an abstract painting. And your grandfather's grave is not the answer because a small forest can make it disappear. Remaining as a neighbor to the rock is also not a satisfactory answer because your alienation is not only material. They have occupied not only land and labor, but also your psychology and temperament and your ties to your homeland until you have started to ask what homeland means. The pursuit of daily life and its cares sometimes keep you from remembering that you really are occupied. Are you a second-class citizen? That is not the question. In your case, it is not only a matter of democracy or humanity. And the tortures you feel do not arise from your own behavior.

"Keep quiet and stay safe" is not innocent advice. It is a call to shake from your hands the soil of the homeland for which you do not find a name. They pulled the earth from under your feet, and you hid inside your skin. They tortured you, and you confessed only to a love beyond measure for the causes of your torture. Threats on the inside will not rub out your sense of belonging, and promises from the outside will not give you a feeling of safety. You take your cross and carry it to your appointment with suicide. And you do not surrender. The alienation that the passing days bring becomes a truce with the wind in the jangling chains. In prison freedom embraces you, and in prison you also become saturated with the homeland. Fighting back is the answer: when you fight back you belong. And the homeland is this struggle. Between memory and the suitcase there is no solution but resistance. Justice, freedom, belonging, and worthiness are only proclaimed through resistance. They were not satisfied to rob you of everything, they also wanted to take away your sense of belonging, so that the battle may rage between you and your homeland and the home-land become a burden, a chain, and a pain. But you will not find freedom outside these chains, and you will not find ease or relief from the burden outside this pain. The homeland that is in your memory and in the cells of your body is entangled with the homeland in their fists and their "return-ing" suitcases.

Journal of an Ordinary Grief

❧

I

—Bend down my love till the storm passes.

—All this bending down has turned my back into a bow. When are you going to release your arrow?
   [You reach one hand out to the other, and find a handful of flour]

—Bend down my love till the storm passes.

—All this bending down has turned my back into a bridge. When will you cross?
   [You try to move your feet, but the iron does not budge]

—Bend down my love till the storm passes.

—From all this bending down my back has turned into a question mark. When will you answer?

[The interrogator plays a record on which there is a burst of applause]

When the storm dispersed them, the present was shouting at the past: "It's your fault." And the past was transforming its crime into a law. As for the future, it was a neutral observer.

When the storm passed, all this curvature was complete, transformed into a circle whose beginning and end are not known.

II

—Take a break after each moan, and tell us who you are.

By the time he was conscious again, the blood had dried.

—I'm from the West Bank.

—And why did they torture you?

—There was an explosion in Tel Aviv, so they arrested me.

—And what do you do in Tel Aviv?

—I'm a construction worker.

The state of affairs in which Arab laborers from the West Bank or the Gaza Strip worked in Israeli cities had not yet become a general condition.

Immediately after the last defeat, Arab public opinion expected the Arab laborer to starve in order to maintain steadfastness and rejection of the occupation. No one in a position of responsibility, however, had thought about the question of securing a means of livelihood for those under occupation so that they could continue in their steadfastness and refusal to cooperate with the conquerors.

—When the guns are silent, don't I have the right to feel hungry?

What do you say to someone who poses the question this way? We do not have the power to grind national anthems and rousing speeches, knead them, and turn them into bread.

It is most dangerous for the homeland under occupation to turn into a loaf of bread. It is also terrible that the population living under military occupation should be forced to go hungry due to the present circumstances of political and military silence.

—During a state of war when battles are raging, we do not think much about the quality of life. Declare a war or fight a battle and we will make all the necessary sacrifices. But when the guns are quiet, we have the right to feel hungry.

And why do we forget, or pretend to forget, that Israel itself was built with Arab hands?

What a paradox! And what a shame!

III

They offer you a red apple, and ask, "Have you tasted Syrian apples?"

How delicious apples are in prison! It is the only thing that transforms the color of ashes into the color of fire.

You say to them: "Syrian apples have invaded Israeli markets, they are bigger, more beautiful, and cheaper. The Jews buy them without batting an eyelid, in spite of protests from the kibbutzim, which are forced to reduce the price of their own apples.

—What brought you here, Syrian brothers? We were preparing to meet you at home in Damascus, and not in prison.

—They arrested us and charged us with stealing back into Quneitra.

—Every return is an infiltration. This is the luck of the Arabs.

—They said we came in order to spy.

—Spying on the houses and the orchards?

—Something like that.

—And did they charge you with stealing your own apples?

—They have not charged us yet.

—How long have you been under arrest?

—Eleven months, one week, and three days.

All of a sudden they ask:

—You know them. Do you think they will charge us with being Syrian?

—Are you not Syrian?

—Yes. We're Syrian.

—Is that what you're charged with?

—We don't know.

IV

—Where are you from, brother?

—From Gaza.

—What did you do?

—I threw a grenade at the conquerors' car, but I blew myself up instead.

—And . . .

—They arrested me, and charged me with attempted suicide.

—You confessed, of course.

—Not exactly. I told them the attempted suicide didn't succeed. So they liberated me out of mercy, and sentenced me to life.

—But you were intending to kill, not to commit suicide?

—It seems you don't know Gaza. Distance there is an imaginary thing.

—I don't understand.

—It seems you don't know Gaza. Where are you from?

—From Haifa.

—And what did you do?

—I threw a poem at the conquerors' car, and it blew them up.

—And . . .

—They arrested me, and charged me with mass murder.

—You confessed, of course.

—Not exactly. I said that the attempted murder succeeded. That is why they showed mercy in responding to my request and sentenced me to two months in prison.

—I don't understand.

It seems you don't know Haifa. Distance there is an imaginary thing.

The prison guard came, put him in prison, and released me.

V

Go. And come back again, while I return to myself from ecstasy.

Stay away till the dream leaves my body.

I taught you to smoke. And you taught me the companionship of smoke.

Go. And come back again!

—And what else did you say to her?

—I didn't talk of love. My words were vague, and I didn't understand them until she slept. She used to sing a lot, and I didn't understand her songs except in dreams. And she's beautiful! Beautiful! The moment I saw her, the clouds lifted from my mind. I snatched her away to my house and said, "Consider this love."

She laughed. Even in the darkest hour she laughed.

I used to call her by a borrowed name because that is more beautiful. When I kissed her I was so full of desire between one kiss and another that I felt I would lose her if we stopped kissing.

Between sand and water, she said, "I love you."

And between desire and torture, I said, "I love you."

And when the officer asked what she was doing here, she answered, "Who are you?" And he said, "And who are you?"

She said, "I'm his sweetheart, you bastard, and I've come with him all the way to the gate of this prison to say goodbye. What do you want with him?"

He said, "You should know that I'm an officer."

"I too will be an officer next year," she said.

She brought out her military induction papers. The officer then smiled, and pulled me away to prison.

The following year the [1967] war erupted, and I was put in prison again. I thought of her: "What is she doing now?" She may be in Nablus, or another city, carrying a light rifle as one of the conquerors, and perhaps at this moment giving orders to some men to raise their arms or kneel on the ground. Or perhaps she is in charge of the interrogation and torture of an Arab girl her age, and as beautiful as she used to be.

She didn't say goodbye.

And you didn't say: "Go, and come back."

You taught her to smoke, and she taught you the companionship of smoke.

VI

—Shall we write a play together?

—Yes. Let us.

—Shall we look for a point we can agree on?

—Yes. Let us.

—Shall we state the case most clearly?

—Yes. Let us.

—Let a house whose ownership is in dispute be the basis of the plot.

—Okay.

—Shall we meet in a month?

—Yes. Let us.

At that moment in the refugee camp, Khadija was saying goodbye to her son, having handed him the key to the house in Haifa known as the "Red House."

At that moment, Sarah, who was living in the "Red House," was saying goodbye to her son, who had just heard an announcement on the radio to join his military unit.

The two young men approach each other from opposite directions and meet in a forest somewhere, and fight. It is not important to know who killed the other.

—Have you finished your chapter?

—I have. "In exile my father didn't teach me despair or suicide, and he didn't teach me to give up my Jewish identity. He brought me up to believe I was born to be pursued. Yet, even so, he did teach me life."

—And you, what have you written?

—"In exile my father didn't teach me despair or suicide, and he didn't teach me to give up my Palestinian identity. He brought me up to believe I was born to be pursued. Yet, even so, he did teach me life."

—This is an important point of agreement.

—And this house that polarizes our destinies, is it a point of meeting, or farewell?

—It's a point of conflict.

—How does the play resolve this conflict?

—Let us say: "The right of ownership does not derive from inheritance, but from need and worthiness. On that basis, the man who built this house fifty years ago does not hold the right to it now because when he left it – no matter under what circumstances – he as much as gave up his need for it.

As for the current owner, he has exerted some effort to take possession of it because he has no other.

—And where is justice in this play?

—Justice. Justice. Let us then look for justice together at this time. Let's make the feeling of guilt prevail in the house until time has taken its desired effect. Let this feeling of guilt on the part of the Jew be a compensation for the loss of the house on the part of the Arab.

—Shall we meet again in a few months to allow me to propose a more just justice?

—Yes. Let us.

At that moment, there were other houses in other cities that were changing dwellers. New keys were piling up over old keys in the Arab places of refuge that were shrinking after each war. At night young men take their house keys and do not return.

VII

—Why this arrogance? I have inherited my religion and ethnicity. It was never a question of choice. Now let me ask you, Who among you has chosen to be a Jew? Who?

—This is the difference between you and me. I'm not simply a Jew: I have chosen to be one.

—How?

—The issue is not subject to discussion. Jewishness can be understood only by Jews. That is the source of my pride that you call arrogance.

—I can understand that you have chosen to be a Zionist, or an Israeli. Is that what you mean?

—Not exactly. I mean that I have chosen my Jewishness and have remained faithful to it.

—And how does this faithfulness manifest itself?

—In the historical homeland.

—And what is this historical homeland? Is it vague, like your identity? Have you chosen, or inherited, it?

—It's vague and clear at the same time. I have chosen and inherited it at once.

The speaker was a writer who rebelled against the distinctions that some people drew between Jewishness, Zionism, and Israeliness. He believed that Jewishness can only manifest in Zionism, and Zionism cannot be realized except in Israeliness. From this perspective, renouncing Zionism means forgoing Jewishness. And when you ask him what the historical homeland means in reality, he reminds you of the famous dialogue that took place between Ben-Gurion and an Arab thinker in 1936, when Palestine was still a Zionist dream. When Ben-Gurion was asked what was the "historical homeland," he answered that it was the territory open to Jewish settlement.

—What is the territory?

—The Land of Israel.

—What are its borders?

—The borders of the Land of Israel are known from history.

—Borders are artificial things. They could be here one day, and over there tomorrow.

—The Land of Israel is that which lies between the Mediterranean Sea in the west and the desert in the east, between Sinai in the south and the source of the Jordan in the north.

—You include Transjordan as well?

—Of course. The Jordan is not a border for the Land of Israel. It's a river within the Land of Israel.[15]

Chaim Weizmann used to say, "I know that God promised the Land of Israel to the children of Israel, but I don't know the boundaries allotted by the Lord."

At that time millions of Arabs used to laugh in mockery of Weizmann and Ben-Gurion. When today you consider the secret boundaries "allotted by the Lord" that go beyond Palestine, you realize that "Israeli reality" is "larger than the Zionist dream" and Jewish history, and remember the writer who said to you, "This is the difference between you and me. I'm not simply a Jew: I have chosen to be one."

Will you laugh again, as the Arabs laughed fifty years ago, or will you hand down your dreams to the children born under the bayonets of the Occupation?

VIII

You want to have fun in the street?

—Darling, on my birthday, I want my present to be a tank or a cannon, or any weapon of Russian make.

—I'll give you a tank where we can sleep together, my dear, so we can try a new position.

—No. We'll sleep together in the open air, on the banks of the Suez Canal.

—Ha! Ha! Ha!

—Ha! Ha! Ha!

You walk in the street, and sit in a coffeehouse. You travel in a bus, and hold your tongue. You are not called upon to declare your identity. Your silence says everything. This is the only stance you can take when you hear this Israeli love talk. The age of sweet words is now over. I'll give you a moon or a gazelle as a present. No. How great the distance between the imagination that roams in the desert and the imagination manufactured by technology and victory! Love talk is now in harmony with the latest events and the most recent technological innovations. Excitement is not in tune now with the things of nature.

Thus the Arab in Israel is now backward even in making love. He needed a long time to know how to address his sweetheart with roses. How many ages, then, will this creature need now to train himself for this kind of love talk. Darling, I'll give you a tank as a present.

And what are you thinking about? About how they sleep together in tanks! And how they give birth to children in tanks? And how they have a good time in their tanks. Go easy now! This is the secure Israeli house. This is the love nest. And it is the future!

IX

What do you do on New Year's Day?

You go down to the street in search of a beautiful greeting card to send to a friend, and what do you find? Not a single picture of a rose, and no drawing of coastline, bird, or woman. All these have disappeared to make room in these cards for the tank, the cannon, the jet fighter, the Wailing

Wall, the occupied towns, and the waters of the Suez Canal. And when you do chance upon an olive branch, you find it painted on the wing of a jet fighter made in France.

When you see a beautiful girl, you find her armed to the teeth. And when your eyes fall upon a city, you find a soldier's boot in the background. Your heart drops to the ground. Nothing is left, except to shrink in a corner of the crowded street to allow room for the thousands of hands stretched toward these colorful holiday cards, to be sent to Jews around the world in celebration of the historical rebirth and the return of the legend. But you do not send anything to your friends except the heart's silence, which does not reach its destination.

The carnival atmosphere in the street catches you by surprise. Light descends upon you as it did when you came out of a darkened cell, and upon multitudes of children/doves armed to the teeth. Toys are weapons. And pleasure is a weapon.

And you? There is nothing in your childhood or your youth except a wooden horse.

X

You want to sleep?

At four in the morning the doorbell wakes you up. You know the visitor, but sleep is more powerful than the police. At nine in the morning you go to work in your office. You enjoy half a cup of coffee before you read the news. The usual visitor comes and says, "Come with me." You ask, "Arrest, or interrogation?" He answers, "I don't know." You ask him to let you bring a toothbrush, shaving equipment, and underwear. He tells you there's no time.

You sit facing the officer.

He says politely, sitting under a photograph of Herzl, "I'm honored to put you under arrest."

You exchange pleasantries, "And I'm honored to grant this honor. But would you kindly tell me what am I accused of?"

He says, "You are accused of exploding a watermelon at the entrance to the circus and threatening the security of the state."

The watermelon, the circus, and the state – a rare concord!

The legal limit of detention is reached. Everything here is according to the law. You expect that you are going to be brought before a judge, and from behind the bars of the police van you enjoy your self-indulgent city. Or you go to an extreme in the exercise of hope, and expect them to release you.

—Wait a little.

You protest, citing the very letter of the law, but they reassure you, "We won't detain you even for an hour after your period of detention is over. What do you think? There is law here. This is Israel, not the Arab world."

You imagine the Arab countries, and choke upon your dreams. And you wait. What are you waiting for? The interrogating officer, or the Arab world?

They lead you into the interrogation room, where you find an officer and an old woman. The officer asks if you can speak Hebrew, then he reads the list of charges: You are accused of plotting to destroy the State of Israel. You ask, "Do you mean the state or the watermelon?" The repulsive woman then says, "Respect the court." You announce your surprise, "Which court?" A voice reaches you as if coming from a swamp: "This is a court, and I am the judge." Then you realize that they have shown you respect, and for your sake had moved the courtroom to the prison. But you refuse to honor them in return, "No, madam. This is not a courtroom, and you are not a judge. This is a prison, and you are the warden."

The session ends with them renewing the period of detention.

XI

You return home in a taxi.

You speak with the driver in fluent Hebrew. Your shape does not announce your identity. "Where to, sir?" asks the driver. "To al-Mutanabbi Street," you reply.

You light a cigarette for yourself and one for him because he is polite. All of a sudden he says, "Tell me, how long must we tolerate this crap? We're sick of it."

You think he is talking about the state of war, the hike in taxes, and the price of bread, and you say, "You are right. It is sickening." Then he continues, "How long will the state persist in keeping these dirty Arabic names? We must get rid of them and erase their names." "Who are they?" you ask. "The Arabs of course," he says in disgust. You ask him why, and he says, "Because they are dirty."

You realize from his accent that he is from Morocco. You ask him, "Am I so dirty? Are you cleaner than me, for example?"

He asks in surprise, "What do you mean?"

You ask him to think about it, and he understands but does not believe. "Stop joking!" he says.

When he sees your identity card, he believes that you are Arab. He says, "I don't mean the Christians." You say that you're a Muslim. Then he says, "I don't mean all Muslims. I mean only those from the villages." You tell him that you are from a backward village that was destroyed by his state and wiped off the face of the earth, as he had wished." And he says, "All respect to the state!"

You get out of the taxi and decide to return home on foot. You are possessed by a fit of reading street names. In fact, they have wiped away their names. Salah al-Din Street has become Shlomo Street. Then you wonder, "Why did they keep al-Mutanabbi's name?" But when you reach al-Mutanabbi Street, you read its name in Hebrew for the first time and realize it has become "Mont Nevi" and not al-Mutanabbi, as you had imagined.

XII

You want to travel to Jerusalem.

You lift the telephone receiver and call the officer in charge of special cases at the police station. You know him well, and you ask about his health and joke with him. Then you ask him politely to give you a travel permit to go to Jerusalem for one day, with no overnight privilege. He says, "Submit a request in writing." You leave your workplace and submit a request on glossy paper. You wait for the response. One day, two days, three days. There is hope because they did not say no as usual. You wait as your appointment in Jerusalem approaches. You ask them, you implore them, and you plead with them to give you some kind of response, even if it is a no, in order to cancel your appointment. They do not say anything. You tell them you have a limited time left before the interview. They say, "Come get it in an hour."

You go, and find the office closed. You ask innocently, "Why are they so polite to me? Why don't they just say no as usual?" You get angry and decide – stupidly – to take revenge on the "security of the state," and you take your trip anyway.

The following day they summon you before a hasty military tribunal. Waiting for your turn, you hear these stories: An Arab woman who works in a kibbutz carries a permit that forbids her to get off the bus at any station on the road. One time she had no choice but to leave the bus, and they arrested her. Some young men took a side road, and they arrested them. No one is ever judged to be innocent in this court. The accused are sentenced to prison terms or made to pay fines. Then you remember the case of the old man, the donkey, and the permit. The man was plowing and had hung his cloak on a tree with his permit in the pocket. He saw that his donkey had strayed from the field onto someone else's land. He ran after it but was stopped by the military police. They arrested him because he had entered state land without a permit. He said, "I do have a permit. It's in the pocket of my cloak hanging in the tree." He was arrested nevertheless, and sentenced.

Then you remember the death permits the farmers had to sign making them responsible for their own death, should a bomb happen to explode while they were in a military zone used for maneuvers. This permit exempts the state from responsibility for their death. But the fellahin had to make a living, and paid no heed to death. And indeed, some of them did die, and some lived. But the state got fed up with both the living and the dead and confiscated the land.

And you also remember the child who died in her father's arms in front of the military governor's door. The father was waiting for a permit to travel from his village to the city, where he could have his sick child treated.

As a result, you feel happy because you received only a two-month sentence. You sing for the homeland, read articles about the homeland, and send letters to your sweetheart. And you read the novel *Freedom or Death*, but you still do not liberate yourself, and you do not die.[16]

XIII

You want to travel to Greece?

You ask for a passport, but you discover you are not a citizen because your father or one of your relatives had fled with you during the Palestine War. You were a child, and you discover that any Arab who had left his country during that period and had stolen back in had lost his right to citizenship.

You despair of the passport and ask for a laissez-passer. You find you are not a resident of Israel because you have no certificate of residence. You think this is a joke and rush to tell to your lawyer friend: "Here, I'm not a citizen, and I'm not a resident either. Then where and who am I?" You are surprised to find the law is on their side, and you must prove you exist. You ask the Ministry of the Interior, "Am I here, or am I absent? Give me an expert in philosophy, so that I can prove to him I exist."

Then you realize that philosophically you exist but legally you do not.

You consider the law. How innocent we were to think the law is a vessel for rights and justice! The law here is a vessel for what the ruler wants, or a suit that he orders to his own measure. I have been in this country even before the state that negates my existence came into being. You realize once again that justice is a hope that resembles an illusion if it is not supported by power and that power transforms the illusion into a reality, and then you smile at the law that grants every Jew in the world the right of citizenship.

Then you try again. You surrender your fate to God and to the law. You obtain a certificate that proves you exist, and you do eventually obtain a laissez-passer, but the question is, "How are you going to pass?" You are in Haifa, and the airport is near Tel Aviv. You ask the police for a permit to pass from Haifa to Tel Aviv and they refuse. The lawyer intervenes, and some members of the Knesset, but the police still refuse. You think you will be more clever and devious than they are, and decide to leave by way of the sea at the Port of Haifa on the understanding that you have the right to pass to the port. You rejoice at your cleverness. You buy a ticket, and you pass through passport control, the health department, and customs without any hindrance. Then, when you are close to the ship, they arrest you and take you to court. This time, you insist that the law is on your side.

But in court you discover that the Port of Haifa is part of the State of Israel, and not part of the city, and they remind you that you are forbidden to be in any part of Israel outside Haifa, and the port according to the law is outside the city. You are found guilty.

You say to them: "Gentlemen, now that I understand the law, I want to make a dangerous confession. I swim in the sea every day, which belongs to the State of Israel and not the city of Haifa, and I do not have a permit to enter the sea."

I have another confession as well: "I enjoy the weather in the city of Haifa, and the weather belongs to the State of Israel and not the city of Haifa. I do not have a permit to enter the weather because the sky I see above me does not belong to Haifa, and I do not have a permit to sit under the sky.

Then you ask for a permit to live in the wind, and they smile.

XIV

You want to celebrate your birthday?

Ah, the celebrations! History attacks you cruelly. One defeat follows another, yet the Arabs celebrate all their holidays. You wonder: "The days erase our days due to all the holidays and occasions. Is there a single day left in the calendar for a victory? All the days are reserved for coups and countercoups, and all of them are official holidays: there you find a reason for your never-ending defeats. But if you were to find an open day in the calendar, then we would be victorious."

Tonight is your birthday: the thirteenth of March. And you want an occasion to wrest a deceptive happiness from the grim days. You gather your friends. You conspire against sadness with cups and music and cutting jokes. The music gets louder and you dance. The laughter of the girls reaches the neighbors' windows. At midnight a policeman arrives. He checks identities and threatens arrest. Be civilized. Enough barbarism. You ask him why, and he says the neighbors had called, to keep the building quiet. You say, "It's a birthday," and he answers, "That's no concern of mine."

Oh my good neighbors! Why didn't you warn me that my happiness gives you pain? And why does the music you play, which is made from my blood, pour into my windows every night with no complaint from me? When are you going to get out of my craw, O neighbors? When?

When you go to bed you reach the conclusion that the neighbors were right. In the morning you apologize: "I have no right to celebrate as long as I am your neighbor. Forgive me, O neighbors!" I repent for celebrating.

XV

You want to rent an apartment?

You read the advertisements in the newspapers, and jump to the telephone: "Madam, I saw the ad for your apartment. Can I see it?"

Her laughter reaches you, full of happiness, and you are filled with hope: "It's an excellent apartment, sir, on Mount Carmel. Come and reserve it right away."

You forget to pay for the phone call, and rush to see her. The lady likes you and you agree on the conditions of payment and the time when the rental begins. And when you sit down to sign the contract, a thunderbolt strikes her on the head. "What! An Arab! Excuse me, sir. Call again tomorrow."

The story is repeated for several weeks. Each time you return empty-handed, you look at the balconies of the houses and ask about their owners, absented by the winds of emigration and exile. How many a house was built by an owner who did not live in it? The owners of these homes still keep their keys in their pockets and their hearts full of anticipation for their return. Return to where? If one of them were to return to his home, will he be allowed to use his key? Will he be able to rent a room in the house he built? On top of all this, they say to you, "Zionism did not commit any crimes. All there is to it is that it brought a people without a homeland to a homeland without a people."

You ask them who built these houses. Then they leave you alone, and bring more children into the world in stolen homes.

XVI

You want to visit your mother on a feast day?

For several long months you have not visited your mother and father and brothers in a village that is no more than an hour's distance away. This time you make a real effort to choose your words in the letter you send to the police. You write, "Please take into consideration the sincerity of the human feelings that lie behind this request and my hope that you will not see in them anything that goes against the careful efforts you exert in guarding the security of the State and in fulfilling the requirements for defending the safety of the public. In seeking your assent for a permit to visit my family during the holidays, I am hoping that you will see the point that the security of the State does not in the slightest degree contradict human feelings."

Your friends leave the city, and you remain behind to drink your coffee and feel sad all alone. There will be family reunions everywhere tomorrow, and you have no right to go to anyone's home. You are left yourself.

The solution lies in the sea. Early in the morning you head for the beach to put out your fire in the blue water. The waves draw you away and do not carry you back. You have to return on your own. In solitude you lie on the warm sand in the open air. Why does the sun squander so much of its energy, and why do the waves break? There is a huge amount of sun, a huge amount of sand, and a huge amount of water. All around you people speak a language you understand, but your sadness and your loneliness and your alienation intensify. A desire possesses you to describe the sea to your girl-friend, but you feel lonely. With reason, or without, they curse your people, yet they enjoy what your people have left behind. Even while swimming or joking or kissing they damn your people. Is the sea not capable of granting them a single moment of innocence and affection so that they can forget about you for a moment? How can human beings feel hate while they are stretched out on the sand? Saturated with sun, salt, and longing you head for the beach snack bar. You drink a beer and whistle a sad song, and all eyes turn to you. You busy yourself with lighting a cigarette that has no taste, and you buy an ear of corn and eat it all by yourself. You wish to be able to spend the whole day at the beach in order to forget that it's a feast day and your family is waiting for you. But the time of your daily appointment at the police station is approaching and you remember all that is happening to you. And in the blink of an eye the color of noon, the sea and sky turn even more blue. Then you leave.

At the entrance to the police station your younger brother is waiting. "Hurry up!" he says. "Prove you exist quickly. Your mother is waiting for you in your room." You forget your pen and paper and hasten back, short of breath. Your mother has refused to eat the holiday meal without you and has come to see you, bringing the food with her from the village, even the coffee and the straw-basket tray full of bread. She has even brought olive oil, salt, and condiments.

When your mother bids you farewell in the evening, you close the door behind her. You cannot accompany her even to the street because the sun has set, and the State of Israel does not allow you to leave the house after sunset, even if the reason is to say goodbye to your mother. On this day of celebration, you feel your loneliness once more. You sit in an ancient chair, and you listen to a concerto by Tchaikovsky, and all of a sudden you start crying as you had never cried when you were a child.

For many years you have been carrying these tears that are pouring down now. Dear Mother, I'm still a child! I want to carry my sorrows and run with them to your bosom. I want to close the distance so you can hold me while I cry.

All of a sudden your neighbor calls out to you, to let you know your mother is still standing at the door. You open it, and fulfill your wish of crying in her arms.

XVII

Sometimes they arrest you while you are committing a dream.

If you thought carefully, you would not have found another accusation, for this writing and those speeches are nothing more than one of the manifestations of the dream in words. What difference is there then in the eyes of the law between the silent dream and the one that roars?

—You were planning to say something else.

—You were planning to do something else.

You are always surprised that you are ready to answer to a charge that you do not know. And if someone else does not accuse you, you will accuse yourself.

—What have you done for the sake of anything?

—What can you do for the sake of anything?

On Saturday you go up Mount Carmel and you never catch up with the dawn. You are surprised by the rare relationship between prison and the sun. This sun – when did you see it being born for the first time? Do not lie and say you searched for it at a picnic or in battle. They woke you up at an early hour and put manacles around your wrists again. Then they took you out to the prison courtyard. And there you witnessed the birth of the sun for the first time. Do not lie, and do not say it was not beautiful, and that you felt ashamed.

On Saturday you go up the mountain. No, this is not a mountain, for Mount Carmel is God's minaret. On the horizon appear trees that camouflage antiaircraft guns and beauty. If a muezzin were to come up and whisper the call to prayer, all the mosques of Damascus would be full of people praying. Lovers and soldiers pass by: "Were the house and the village and the life that we created here – were they so dear and real and right before now?" So they ask after war and victory. And you ask the same question. They say, "With every step on the earth here the shadows retreat, and greenness and hope take possession of you." And after war and defeat you say, "With every step on the earth here my heart falls, and greenness and hope and conquerors take possession of me."

They place you under arrest while you are committing a dream.

—What would you have done had the Arabs won the war?

You answer, "I would have gone up the mountain, chosen a pine tree, and sat. Then I would have stretched my feet out to the Mediterranean. I would have touched the hair of the sky and followed the dream exactly as I am doing now.

—But that is not how victors behave.

—I have never once been the victor, to know how victors behave.

You feel you are no longer a citizen. Your history is nothing more than dreams that are torn to pieces like a newspaper, and each dream is a disaster.

What use to you are Yarmouk and Qadisiya and other historical battles? And why you? Why you? Beautiful is Carmel, and close is the sky, and far away is victory. And what have you done for the sake of anything? Nothing. You find yourself outside war, outside victory, outside defeat, and outside your own humanity.

Accordingly, you become a tree or a stone or any natural thing.

He Who Kills Fifty Arabs
Loses One Piaster

❧

Here they lie. Their names were many, and their death was one. They were tired, and sunset came quickly. They fell to the ground with ease and without saying anything because the appointed time had come suddenly. What if they had been told? They knew what was required. The whole family was returning home from work, but the world was not for them.

Here they lie. They were punished for an obscure crime. They did not take part in a demonstration, and did not defend life and soil except with prayer. They used to leave their misery early in the morning, and return to it before sunset. They were waiting for rain, but death fell on them like a heavy rain.

Here they sleep. The sunset grows larger and changes into forests of dry trees. There is no hour to commemorate their death, no occasion, and no appointment. The stones themselves are time, and the expanse of the pale sunset is time. What name shall we give them?

The Kufr Qasem Massacre is not a day for remembrance, and it is not a passing phase that forgetfulness will defeat. It is rather the history of a hatred that began from the moment Herzl drew his sword out of the Torah and brandished it in the face of the Orient. The inhabitants of this downtrodden and neglected village did not engage in anything that should rouse anyone's anger, even the ones who had volunteered to be the enemy. They fought only against harsh nature and black despair. Why then did they die? They did not die for our sake at all. They were victims, not martyrs. And that is their twofold tragedy, and the source of our twofold grief over them. We could say that they died so that our hatred of oppression and usurpation would grow deeper and our worship of the land would deepen. We do not need such savage facts. We are perfectly capable of developing our sense of love or hatred without this death for nothing. For what did they die then?

Not for our sake but for that of the killers, so that Zionists may feel they are capable of playing a role in history other than that of victim. Killing tastes delicious when it is done for such an aim. "Either be a killer, or be the one killed" – this is the narrow choice they have set before themselves.

In the court/stage the lawyer interrogates an Israeli soldier who took part in the massacre:

> Lawyer: Is it true that you are working for this country, and that all your life you have felt that the Arabs are our enemies?
> Soldier: Yes.
> Lawyer: Is it true that you have these feelings against the Arabs in Israel, as well as the Arabs outside of it?
> Soldier: Yes. I see no difference between them.
> Lawyer: Is it true you felt that if you hadn't carried out the order

to kill all Arabs in Kufr Qasem who were outside their homes, then you would have felt you had betrayed the spirit instilled in you in the Army and the Border Guard?

Soldier: Yes.

Lawyer: If, during the [1956] war, you were walking in a street in say, Jaffa, and you ran in to an Arab, would you have shot him?

Soldier: I don't know.

Judge: Suppose you had the following experience in Kufr Qasem. After 5 p.m. a woman calls out to you, and you are certain she is not dangerous and does not threaten the security of the state. She wants to ask a question, or ask for permission to pass to her house, and let us say that this takes place at 5:20. Supposing this woman was only ten meters away from her house and she asked you for permission to go into it, what would you have done?

Soldier: I wouldn't have allowed her.

Judge: What would you have done?

Soldier: If she were in the street, I would've shot her.

Judge: But you were not in any danger. All that happened was that a certain person, because of a certain mistake, who did not know about the curfew order, came forward and asked for permission to cross the street, the question is then, would you still have killed everyone, or would you have refrained from killing in certain circumstances?

Soldier: I wouldn't have made any distinctions.

Judge: Would you have killed everyone?

Soldier: Yes.

Judge: Even if that person were a woman or a child?

Soldier: Yes.

Judge: You would have killed everyone you had seen?

Soldier: Yes.

And that was what actually took place.

The goat of Talal Shaker Issa, a child of eight, had run away from the courtyard into the street. Neither the child nor the goat understood that the curfew order had just gone into effect in the village a few hours before. The child ran after the goat, and the bullets fell upon him like rain and killed him.

His father followed, and the rifle carried on with its mission.

The wife ran toward her husband and her son, and the rifle continued with its mission. Their daughter, Noura, followed her parents and her brother, and the rifle still continued with its mission.

Now what was the mission of that rifle?

On the eve of the tripartite attack on Egypt in 1956, the brigade commander Colonel Shadmi called the battalion commander Major Malinki to his headquarters and gave him the orders for the unit under his command. The Border Guard was charged with the imposition of a total curfew that kept the villagers living in Kufr Qasem and the other villages in the Central Area restricted to their homes from five in the evening till six in the morning. The following exchange took place between the two commanders, which is now part of the District Court record:

> Shadmi: The curfew must be absolute, and maintained with a strong arm, not just by arresting those who don't observe it, but by shooting them. It's better to kill them than have to deal with the complications that follow upon arrest.

Malinki: What will be the fate of citizens who know nothing about the curfew if they should run into the Border Guard on their way home from outside the village?

Shadmi: I don't want any sympathy. God have mercy on their souls!

At the end of this quick and decisive exchange, Malinki issued an order to the captain of the reserves attached to his platoon that contained the following: "No dweller is permitted to be outside his house during the curfew. He who leaves his house is to be shot, and there will be no arrests."

The following exchange took place between Malinki and his soldiers, as can be determined from the records of the District Court:

Soldier: What shall we do with the wounded?

Malinki: There should be no concern with them. They must not be moved. There will be no wounded.

A platoon leader asked: What about women and children?

Malinki: No emotions!

Same platoon leader: What about those who are coming back from work?

Malinki: They get the same treatment as all the rest. These are the leader's orders. May God have mercy on their souls!

On the same day at half past four in the afternoon, only half an hour before the curfew was to begin, a sergeant from the Border Guard informed the village elder of Kufr Qasem that the curfew would be going into effect that afternoon, starting at five and lasting till six in the morning. He cautioned the elder that the curfew would be observed strictly, with danger of death, and asked that he announce that to the village. The elder informed him that at that moment there were four hundred workers from Kufr Qasem at their places of work outside the village. Some of them worked nearby, while others were in distant places, like Jaffa and Lydda, and it would be impossible for him to notify them about the curfew with such short notice. After some discussion the sergeant promised that he (and the government) would assume the responsibility of allowing them to pass through when they returned from work.

So under his own authority and that of the government, forty-nine Arab citizens of the village of Kufr Qasem were shot down by the Border Guard. Among these were seven boys and girls and nine women.

Ten years after the massacre that satisfied Israeli thirst for unarmed Arab blood, Saleh Khalil Issa, who had miraculously escaped death, related to the poet Tawfiq Zayyad his eyewitness account:

> On that day I was working with two of my cousins in an orchard. We finished work a little after four. We got on our motor scooters and headed for the village. On the way we met some other workers who said they heard the village was under curfew, that there were shootings and no one knew why. The number was growing until there were twenty-five workers. After some hesitation we decided to continue on our way home until we were within one kilometer of the village. We had no serious fears. One thing I worried about was running into Blum, the Border Guard captain, and that he would curse us and deliver some blows as usual. Nothing else was on my mind.
>
> In a while we heard shooting. I began to sense that danger was at hand and said to my cousin, "Let's go back," but he encouraged me to

go on. There was a sheikh with us, around sixty years old, and he also encouraged us with verses from the Qur'an. We came closer until we were about one hundred meters from the nearest house in the village.

All of a sudden a man from the Border Guard appeared and blocked our way: "Halt!" Even till that moment I was expecting to be beaten, but not to be killed.

We got off our scooters, and the soldier ordered us to stand in line:

"Where are you from?"

"From Kufr Qasem," we all said in one voice.

"Where were you?"

"At work."

He moved about five meters away, where there were two of his colleagues with machine guns, and shouted:

"Mow them down!"

I couldn't believe it was happening until I heard the bullets pouring in our direction. The first wave was at aimed our feet; the second a little higher. I fell to the ground with the others. Next to me was a horse cart whose owner they had detained and shot along with us. I fell behind the cart, I don't know how. I felt I was alive only after I had fallen. That is all. The three soldiers then moved till they were ten meters away.

In a few moments a truck arrived. They stopped it and ordered the people riding in the back to come down. There were many people (I later found out there were twenty-three) who were employees of the Osamia agricultural company.

The same soldier who gave the order to shoot us came forward and ordered them to come down and line up behind the vehicle. After they had lined up very close to each other, he moved away from them and shouted:

"Mow them down!"

A few got away but the majority fell. The three killers then came to where I was and the other scooter-riders who were now dead and started to stack them into one pile three meters from where I was. They had heavy guns, and were finishing off the wounded.

They came near, and dragged the horse cart away. Its metal wheel with all its weight rolled over my foot. I clenched my teeth so as not to cry out. I pretended I was dead. They dragged me over to the pile and moved off.

Afterward they put those they had killed from the truck in a pile about ten meters away from us. Another truck arrived, with two people in it. They killed them. Then I heard the noise of a jeep coming down the road from the east, from the direction of the village. The motor was turned off, and I saw someone descending from it. I didn't understand what they were saying to each other, as they were about twenty meters away from me. Then the jeep went back in the direction it came from.

There was a period of quiet.

I saw the three killers walk away and sit at the edge of the village well. Then another truck came. (You might have noticed that they killed each group a few meters away from the preceding group but in the opposite direction so that the new group would not be able to see what happened to the previous one.) But the vehicle I just mentioned passed right by the pile of dead bodies, and it seemed the killers no longer cared whether the new victims saw what happened to the previous ones or not. The vehicle passed to the side of the pile of bodies in the middle of which I was lying.

I heard women's voices. Later I found out there were thirteen women from the age of twelve up, and four men.

Suddenly, the three killers ran behind this car and stopped it. They ordered all the passengers out.

I thought the car was between twenty and twenty-five meters away, and I felt an immense strength taking hold of me. I stood up and started running. I didn't how I jumped a fence that was facing me there. Unconsciously, I ran in a direction parallel to the car. The bullets descended on me like a heavy rain. The sound of the bullets was mixed up with the wailing of the women and the sound of bodies falling to the ground. I felt a bullet penetrate my clothes. Only then did I realize where I was. I fell to the ground and started to crawl in the direction of an olive orchard. I imagined the orchard was full of army and military vehicles, and that I would run into them any moment. I hid behind a big rock under an olive tree, thinking of the death that might overtake me at any moment. I stayed there till morning, my hands and legs bleeding. Two soldiers discovered me, and I was taken to a hospital.

The next morning the criminals searched for a way to bury their crimes. They brought some people from the neighboring village of Jaljuliya to the Kufr Qasem graveyard and ordered them to dig forty-seven graves. Those charged with digging the graves did not know anything about the crime. They had only to dig. That was all. Ever since that day the Kufr Qasem cemetery has grown in stature. It has become a shrine, and clear evidence of the "purity" of Jewish arms in Israel.

The crime did not end with the burial of the dead. The massacre did not stop with the drying blood. So that the operation of killing fulfill its Israeli conditions, it was necessary for the "Israeli conscience" – famous for its sensitivity to any injury that touches any Jew in the world – to lead itself into the temptation of testing its humanity. It was essential that this sensitive conscience be located. It had hitherto been absent – absent because the victims were Arabs. It would seem that the legality of killing Arabs, or indifference to their killing, has become ordinary and taken for granted in Israeli society, brought up on the instinct of hostility to these creatures who muddy the atmosphere of the "purity" of Jewish existence in Palestine. A sadistic, or even a joyful, silence followed the event. There were no exceptions to the rule of silence except for a few writers who were pained by the soiled reputation of the purity of Jewish arms propagated by the apologists for Zionist crimes. The poem by the well-known poet Nathan Alterman was not written in defense of murdered justice as much as it was a defense of the reputation of the usurping Israeli society:

> We cannot write about anything else. We cannot write a story or a poem, because the Hebrew language refuses to pass in silence over this ugly event that took place in Israel.
>
> That is the nature of this language, and its quality.
>
> They say: We will bring the matter to court – and be done with it. The law will speak, and issue its judgment.
>
> They say: Let's leave all this to the law. Is that not enough?
>
> No. That is not enough.
>
> Justice is an exhausted alphabet because it is not possible for the crime to awaken the law.
>
> But, before the trial and after, this case will still be missing a significant principle.

It is not possible for a human society to exist in which this type of cowardice takes place, without a tremor of anger.

A collective anger that expresses the indignation of humanity and the individual.

The indignation of men and women.

Because without this, justice will be nothing more than a mechanical reaction, programmed and automatic.

A reaction that takes place in a vacuum, and not among a people with awakened senses.

The writer Boas Evron demolished the reputed spiritual and moral claims put forth by apologists for the Israeli government. He wrote, "Since the crime, we have been undergoing a test. Our rectitude, our humanity, and our courage have been put to a test which we have failed." He named four guilty parties:

First, the press. With the exception of two or three newspapers, the press took part in a conspiracy of silence and lowered the screen on the event. Instead of writing about the crime of murder in Kufr Qasem, it talked about a "misfortune," or an "offense," or "the regrettable incident." When the press discussed the victims of this misfortune, it was not clear to whom they were referring: the killers or the victims. The second group includes the religious leadership and the general religious milieu in the country. These leaders, who claim authority that "Jewish morality and the spirit of our patriarch

Israel may prevail in the country," were totally silent and completely indifferent. Not even one religious personality rose up to save the honor of Judaism. The third group is the academic leadership. With the exception of a few "crazy ones," there was not a single professor or lecturer who proclaimed, "This is murder." The fourth group includes the literary and artistic leaders. The Association of Writers, which is known for such phrases as "protesting forcefully" or "appealing to the conscience of the enlightened world," was silent, is silent, and will maintain its silence.

The writer adds, "And what about all the ruling parties that all this time have waved the banners of peace, justice, and the brotherhood of nations? Where were the revolutionaries? And where were we, the ordinary citizens who felt insulted and disgusted by the dance of the jinn?"

The dance of the jinn was the trial.

This was the third chapter of the crime that began with the murder, followed by silence, then by the trial. In preparation for the trial, held only after a great deal of prevarication, the government reached an insulting settlement with the relatives of Kufr Qasem's victims.

The Ministry of Defense set aside the sum of one hundred thousand Israeli pounds as the price for the life of fifty Arab victims.

The cheapest price in history.

The valuation was made according to the following scheme: two thousand pounds for someone who is fifteen years old. One thousand pounds is the price for those younger than eight. The price of a married man without children is three thousand pounds. A married man with one child is worth four thousand pounds. A married man with more than one child is worth five thousand pounds. And by recourse to known, and unknown, methods of persuasion, the government was able to impose a settlement and these compensations.

The trial of the killers then began, after the victims had been found guilty!

Two years after the crime was committed, and after a trial that lasted a very long time, the court issued the sentences. How beautiful it is that the military authorities should distribute the roles – from killers, to judges, to witnesses.

In its "just" sentence the court found Major Malinki and Lieutenant Jubrail Dahhan guilty of the murder of forty-three citizens and sentenced the first to a prison term of seventeen years and the second to a term of fifteen years. As for the third defendant, Shalom Ofer, who most horrifyingly committed the greatest number of murders (as documented in Sabri Jiryis's book, citing the rulings of the District Court), he and Dahhan were found guilty of killing forty-one citizens and were given a sentence of fifteen years.[17] The fourth and fifth defendants, Privates Makhlouf Hreish and Eliahu Avraham, were found guilty of killing twenty-two citizens. The sixth, seventh, and eighth defendants – Corporal Jubrail Olel, Privates Albert Fahima and Edmund Nachmani – were found guilty of killing seventeen citizens and, along with the two previously mentioned defendants, each received a sentence of eight years. The court found the remaining three defendants innocent.

These light sentences, which in the final analysis meant the encouragement of more murders under the cover of judicial leniency, astounded the Arab citizens and raised their level of worry about their future. At the same time, these sentences raised the level of indignation of Jewish extremists in Israel, who claimed that the killers were only doing their national duty. Some Israeli newspapers did not hesitate to ask for pardon for the killers.

It was not astonishing, or surprising, that Israeli officials should respond positively to these popular demands. The Supreme Court of Military Appeals found that the sentences handed down for the killers were too harsh and it was necessary to reduce them. The Court then lowered Malinki's sentence to fourteen years, Dahhan's to ten years, and Ofer's to nine years. Then the chief of staff interfered in the matter and further reduced Malinki's sentence to ten years, Dahhan's to eight, and that of the rest of the killers to four.

Then it was the president's turn to demonstrate in depth the principles of justice of Israeli murder, and he granted partial pardon to Malinki and Dahhan by reducing their sentences to five years.

This series of reductions started to look like a tournament of rewards, in which the killers were honored for their success in cold-blooded murder. The Parole Board volunteered to reduce everyone's sentence by a further one-third. Then the murderers were all released at the beginning of 1960. Beyond that, Israeli officials decided that Jubrail Dahhan, who had killed forty-three Arabs in one hour, deserved a civilian job in [the mixed city of] Ramlé, worthy of the blood relationships that connected him with the Arabs, and the municipality announced the same year that it had offered him a position in charge of Arab affairs.

Now what happened to Colonel Shadmi, who gave the orders to Malinki, advising him to issue instructions of "No emotion"? And who was the higher authority from whom Shadmi received his orders? An honest trial of Shadmi would have certainly revealed the highest person in command responsible for the orders, and for that reason Shadmi was tried in a sham military court appointed by the chief of staff.

The trial was over quickly, and the court found that Shadmi had made only a "technical error," and so issued him a rebuke and imposed a fine of one Israeli piaster.

Perhaps Shadmi's piaster is the most costly currency in the history of crime. Its reputation will grow as long as crimes exist on the face of the earth. The man responsible for the death of forty-nine innocent citizens in a peaceful village is punished by having to pay only one piaster. This does not happen frequently. It does not happen frequently in history, unless the victims of Nazism had learned how to imitate their killers. This is the lesson learned by the practitioners of Zionism in the land of Palestine.

And what did the Jewish thinker Ahad Ha'am, who devoted his life to the Zionist mission, fighting against the assimilation of Jews in Eastern Europe, write? What did he write when he saw with his own eyes the behavior of Jewish immigrants to Palestine in 1891, even before they established their state? He wrote: "How do our immigrant brothers behave in Palestine? They were slaves in the lands of the Diaspora, and suddenly found themselves with unbridled freedom. This sudden transformation has engendered in their souls a tendency toward tyranny, as is usually the case when the slave becomes the master. They treat the Arabs with enmity and cruelty, abusing their rights in a twisted and unreasonable manner. They humiliate them without any excuse and, beyond all that, they brag about their actions. There is no one among us who can stand in the way of this dangerous and contemptible tendency."[18] If Ahad Ha'am, the model Zionist, complained about the viciousness of the first immigrants even before they had a state, weapons, and an army, what would it be possible for an observer to write now?

Killing forty-nine Arabs in Kufr Qasem, exonerating their killers, and shunning trial for those who gave the orders because that would have meant passing judgment on Israel itself as now constituted – this was not enough to satisfy the Israeli government's criminal instinct. It was not enough because the government possesses enough sadism and hypocrisy to enable it to blackmail the victims into recognition of its legitimacy and support for its lethal weaponry. By its special means, the Israeli government, immediately after the massacre, was able to extort support for the ruling party in the parliamentary elections: the ruling killer party received the vast majority of votes in the stricken village. The crime thus had a double edge: they killed them, and then forced them to declare allegiance. They cross-examined the corpses until they said yes to the killer conquerors.

The aim of the killers was to depict the massacre as an unfortunate accident, but was it really accidental, or second nature, part and parcel of Zionist behavior in Palestine and a continuing policy toward the Arab citizens who have fallen under Israeli bondage? Deir Yassin they also called an accident, but is an accident still an accident when repeated ten times? Cold-blooded killing and armed violence constitute the Israeli philosophy. Zionist writing has filled many pages giving violence a legitimacy derived from the need to establish Israel and preserve it. We may observe that some liberal Zionists object to violent incidents when the distinction is blurred between violence with political aims and that which is nothing more than a crime based on savage vengeance. This distinction explains the meaning of Ahad Ha'am's famous burst of anger, because objection to Zionist violence, when taken to its logical conclusion, will lead to rejection of the official basis on which Israel was founded, namely, armed violence. But what happened in Kufr Qasem went beyond armed violence, which some may justify on political grounds. This crime was not like the crime committed in Deir Yassin, for example, which the conquerors used to instill terror in the hearts of the Arabs in order to force them to flee, and which did in fact serve the political aims of territorial expansion and victory. The Kufr Qasem crime did not preempt any possible threat to Israeli security, since the laborers and farmworkers of the village and its women and children did not threaten that security or stand in the way of the Israeli army's push toward Sinai.[19] The crime here was planned and executed for no essential reason, if we can put the matter that way. It is a crime committed only for its own sake. It represents the most advanced form of criminality motivated by instincts for killing and vengeance. It was the famous terrorist Menachem Begin who extolled this type of armed violence, when Zionists resorted to it before 1948, as the only effective method of safeguarding the national aims in Palestine, adding that it "satisfied a repressed but overwhelming need for vengeance among the Jews." That was before 1948, so why Kufr Qasem in 1956? Perhaps the philosophy of existence of the terrorist Zionist ("I fight therefore I exist") needs constant practice and demonstration. Perhaps the Zionist Israeli who bears a repressed desire for revenge – as Begin affirms – needs to renew his existence by one means only, which is war, and to fill this existence with a new reason to prove his uniqueness, specifically to kill, kill, kill. "Be my brother, or else I'll kill you," thus adds the philosopher of crime. And since it is impossible for the Arab who lives under Israeli bondage to think of his killer as his brother, the circle of killing never closes.

There is no end in Zionist thought to making excuses for armed violence that finds inspiration in religion. For this reason, Joshua Son of Nun has become a contemporary Israeli hero due to the savagery of the methods he used in dealing with non-Jewish peoples. This savagery, which bears a historical resemblance to current Zionist practice, is needed today by the decision makers in Israel as a source of inspiration and support from tradition for carrying on with the Israeli renaissance in Palestine on the understanding that a crime becomes legal and justified as long as it helps to realize Zionist aims. The situation had gotten so extreme that some "reasonable" Israelis have called for banning instruction about Joshua Son of Nun in the schools because it ruins the minds of young people, making them incapable of getting used to the idea of living in peace with the Arabs in case the state of affairs that currently prevails between Arabs and Jews were to change.

Israel makes a great show of sensitivity to any practice that it sees as oppressive to Jews anywhere in the world, but such practices quickly become legitimate and humane when practiced against the Arabs. And what was considered savagery when directed against Jews quickly changes into a Jewish national duty when undertaken with the "pure" Jewish arms against the Arabs. It was not an Arab who wrote that Zionism "considers any action it carries out correct and just, but wrong if carried out by others." It was Moshe Smilansky who said that Jewish nationalism in Palestine was built on a military egotism that believes in violence and is as far away from human considerations as it can be.

Briefly, then, the crimes that Israel commits against the Arab civilians, of which the Kufr Qasem massacre was a staggering example, do not stem from a "bad" application of the "excellent" Zionist heritage, but rather from an excellent application of the dreadful Zionist heritage. This is precisely the point that stands as a Gordian knot for those who defend the principles of a "spotless" Zionism by merely raising objections to the poor Israeli application of these principles; it will remain an immovable rock facing those who do nothing more than object to Israeli violation of the "sacredness" of Zionist teachings. Any objection to Israeli practice will be meaningless, a way of deceiving oneself and others, if it remains committed to defending the soundness of Zionist ideology.

Zionist heritage and its "clear" spring have legitimized violence and crime. Jabotinsky was honest with himself when he said to the adviser of the Jewish students in Vienna: "You can abolish everything – the cap, the ribbons, the colors, heavy drinking, the songs, everything, but not the sword. You are going to keep the sword. Sword fighting is not a German invention. It belonged to our forefathers. The Torah and the sword were both handed down to us from heaven."[20]

The Zionist challenge is not centered in humanitarian values and cultural confrontation as it claims, but in claiming priority for armed violence and the sword. The rush to adopt these beliefs led another Zionist thinker, Joseph Berdichevsky, to the point of objecting to the pairing of Book and sword: "The Book and the sword contradict and cancel each other out completely. These are very difficult times for the Jewish people. And in times like these men and nations live by the sword and not by the Book. The sword is not something abstract, at a remove from life. It is a material manifestation of life in its purest meanings. The Book is not like that."

Just as we find no end in Zionist thought to the justification of terrorism and violence by appealing to political principles, religious pretexts, and the obsession with historical oppression, we also find no end to these practices in Israeli natural inclination. The first pioneers called for violence, which the soldiers and Border Guard put into practice, while propagandists claim that Israeli arms are the purest and that the Israeli conquerors are the most beautiful. They proved these claims on many occasions and demonstrated how "beautiful and pure" they were in their dealings with the Arab inhabitants, the laborers and children of Kufr Qasem in particular. With a fine of only one piaster the curtain is drawn over the massacre of forty-nine citizens.

When we tried to enter Kufr Qasem to commemorate its victims with the villagers, the same Border Guards, the very killers, put the grieving village under siege, preventing visitors from offering condolences. These heroic killers, why are they afraid of the memory of their victims? It is not feelings of guilt that drive them to the eradication of memory, but hatred, sadism, and a need to prove they exist. Their existence is tied up with the crime, as if they are trying to renew the act of killing every year by eradicating its memory. But we know how to commemorate the victims of the massacre. The Palestinian people know how to avenge their dead: by holding on to the soil of the homeland with their nails and teeth. It says to the conqueror: "We won't sign the letter granting you indulgence." The government continues to commit vengeful acts against this people. This vengeance reached its peak when, on the very day of commemoration of the Kufr Qasem massacre, the government laid the foundation for the city of robbery, Karmiel, on the ruins of three Palestinian villages in the Galilee – this in order to show the Arabs its true intentions toward them, revealing the two edges of its sword: murder on one edge, and confiscation of land on the other.

Kufr Qasem does not hold a significant place in the history of Palestine, and the poetic imagination cannot depict it in glowing colors. But that setting sun, standing watch over the blood about to be shed, made of little-known Kufr Qasem the epic story of an enduring people. One evening, as we stood at the village gates, we felt the sharp pain of the joy pent up within us, and understood the crime for which we have been rewarded with all this punishment. We realized that stones are made of time, and we sat down on them to sing to the homeland.

Happiness – When It Betrays

❧

I

They taught you to be wary of happiness because it hurts when it betrays. But from where did it come all of a sudden?

Time conquers you with memories that do not resemble you. You had just left May 15 behind, and you were not able to attach yourself to things that were far from your pores. The grandfather who had bid you to keep an eye on the hill that looked out on the sources of his death had died. Your brother loves to give speeches. He stood upon the ruins and promised that the next funeral would be luckier than the first one. You had not reached the age of thirty, yet nearness to death had given you wisdom. And wisdom demands that you not show your feelings in public.

The specified period of mourning ends with a travel permit. You sneak away from the second funeral and promise your family you'll be back for the next one, for this is the only occasion that allows you to obtain a permit to travel. How powerful is the tie between motion and death! You had just come out of the fifteenth of May, and you were rushing to get home, not to beat the setting sun but to run away from the fireworks exploding in the streets on the occasion of the nineteenth anniversary of the killing.

What did they say to you last time?

"Knights you are, O Arabs, knights!"

Every night of every year on this date is the day of your suicide, which no one else feels. Often suicide is undertaken just for show. But your suicide takes place in secret. A day descends upon you that pierces your flesh and slowly spreads through your bones like a small continuous earthquake that does not expand or erupt.

The eruption – that is what preoccupies you. You have been waiting for it for twenty years, but then it does not come because your condition cannot be comprehended, and it does not reveal itself. How easy it would be to write a poem that could abort the eruption, and how easy to engage your enemy in a dialogue – to prove what? That you have rights?

And what did they say to you last time?

"Knights you are, O Arabs, knights!"

And if they were to give you everything you wanted, what would you do? Would you be satisfied? Would you stop searching for the source of the eruption? And, can you be secure in your happiness? He who robbed you of everything will not give you anything. And if he did, he would be insulting you. "Be wise, and go back to the soil." That is what you said to yourself, and you did not answer my question, "If they were to give you everything you wanted, could you guarantee your happiness?" You look back on your days and sort the beautiful slogans you carried, walking with them into prison:

Travel permit!

Freedom of expression!

Equality!

Suddenly you laugh. Equality makes you laugh. And you resist, that you may not be secure in your happiness. The days have taught you not to trust happiness because it hurts when it deceives. Where has it come from, then, all of a sudden?

II

You wait for something else.

The condition of waiting is the sole excuse for your belief in demands that remain valid throughout the year but that always reveal their absurdity on the fifteenth of May.

You are not responsible for anything that happened in the past. The past was not made by you, or by any mistakes you made. But it is your heritage. For example, have you been to Tiberias?

You have read Hebrew poetry describing this city overlooking the Sea of Galilee. But you are not permitted to see it. Is your overwhelming desire to see it trivial? And would your resistance be in vain if you fought for a permit to see your cities? No. But you wait. And why do you want to see Tiberias anyway when Arab artillery looks out over it, promising it to you?

You sleep, while the radio lying in your bed is awake. You know the names of all the announcers on Arab radio stations, and you know the schedule for newscasts, for recitations from the Qur'an, and for music and drama. And all of them are beautiful. Everything the Arabs do is beautiful because they are your support. No one objects to the voices of airline hostesses; they are all beautiful while announcing the imminent landing of the plane in any city. All the broadcasts and those working in radio have promised you safe landing in the cities of your dreams. You have no right to know the truth now because the truth might mean the end of your right to wait. And when the critics started to argue about the absurdist identity of Godot, you did not understand what the fuss was all about. You were smarter than all the critics and even Beckett himself, for he who has waited twenty years knows Godot.

Have you been to Caesarea?

You have read Hebrew poetry describing its beautiful golden coastline and you felt elated. When the Arabs you were listening to on the radio made mistakes in pronouncing the names of your cities and villages, you did not get angry or blame them. When you see what the Hebrew guide has done to these names, you forgive the Arabs their errors. You smile at the mistakes of the Arabs like a father smiles at the mistakes of his child as he learns to speak.

Sometimes you used to ask:

"What is the relation between the conquerors and these stones, this water, and these trees?"

You did not remember till later that their political and emotional discourse is attached to these in an astonishing manner, touching on details and things you cannot see. This is not your fault, because from your youth they restricted where you could live, and their writings became the only tool available to you for learning about your homeland. Is that not a strange paradox? Vanity of vanities; all is vanity. Later you remember that one aspect of your resistance is the emotional competition over the love of this land, and not merely over mental claims to it. They have married the claim to sentiment. How? Can the conqueror be in love to such an extent? The French and the Americans did not write love poems for the forests of Vietnam; they died there, but without love. You dread the thought, and fear that drawing such an example might be used as evidence against you, but Algeria saves you. So you calm down, and feel assured about the efficacy of waiting.

Frequently they have said:

"Knights you are, O Arabs, knights. Since your belonging to this land is true and deeply felt, why don't you write poems about the landscape?"

The landscape. What is it? You walk out to the balcony. The evening takes you out of yourself, and the watchman brings you back. From the hole in the police car you give your eyes to the landscape. How can blue and green and orange come together in one vessel without mixing? The colors maintain the independence of their individual beauty as well as their resemblance. Mount Carmel descends to the shore, and the sea begins. The sea ends and the evening begins. The evening ends and the interrogation begins.

—Knights you are, O Arabs, knights!

—Why?

—Because you do not believe in time.

—What do you mean?

—Nineteen years have passed, and your demands are nothing but fancy.

—We learned to believe in fancy from you.

—What do you mean?

—Two thousand years have passed, and your demands are nothing but fancy.

—This is our country.

—And this is our country.

—We are more powerful.

—Knights you are, O Israelis, knights!

—Why?

—Because you do not believe in time.

—What do you mean?

—Might does not make right, and we grow stronger as time passes.

—But it is our country, and we will defend it.

—It is our country, and we will defend it.

—The weapons will decide, then.

—They have decided for you, but not for us yet.

And the June War was just around the corner.

You were waiting.

And they were waiting.

Stay optimistic, and wait for June.

This was the source of your sudden happiness. But the days have taught you to be wary of happiness, because it hurts when it betrays.

III

The ordinary Israeli had reached the point of swinging back and forth between bread and the text. He used to say, I "returned" to the Promised Land to fulfill the historical mission of the great Jewish nation. Under less idealistic circumstances, he would say, I "came" to a safe land to save my skin from Nazi persecution. "Crows have a homeland, but I don't have one." Under more realistic circumstances he would say, "I live" in the Land of Israel and I have no other aim than to be secure and live in peace. But he did not read the proverb that says, "Be just, and live securely and sleep peacefully."

The nationalist feeling among Israelis was less pronounced before June [1967], when they faced the truth of the difference between "the Promised Land" – in the hymns of the vanguard, "the land of milk and honey, and the solution to the Jewish problem" – and the extremely harsh reality in May, when inflation and unemployment reached record heights. Then emigration from, and not immigration to, Israel became the issue of the day. The sense of Jewish irony was revived as Israelis started to say, "Will the last traveler kindly not forget to turn off the lights at Lydda Airport." At that time books that made fun of the prime minister devoured all Zionist nationalist books, for the land of milk and honey had no bread and butter. The ordinary Israeli this time alternated between the body and economic demands, and Israeli newspapers started to accuse the workers on strike of being agents of the Palestinian fedayeen organizations. It then became obvious to the observer that Israeli resentment began to shift from their governing institutions to the borders of the 1948 Arab-Israeli Truce.

Security first, then bread. The Israeli establishment constantly exerts itself to augment Jewish fears in order to help neutralize the economic demands of the people and divert them to the question of war. Israel rushed to fight fiercely under the slogan of "self-defense against the danger of annihilation," while misleading the outside world about their fear of the Arab invasion.

The ordinary man on the street was afraid, afraid, afraid.

Your Israeli friends came to visit you every night, and drank till they were inebriated, as if they were drinking life itself. "Who knows, the war may start tomorrow, and we may never come back." The homeland suddenly became a catastrophe. "Is it for such an end that we came?"

A live Israeli was no longer more important than a dead Jew. And you used to ask, "How could the Israeli establishment inspire the kind of fear you only find onstage?" They were in fact, many of them without knowing it, acting out the drama of those on their way to death. Despair. Despair. Despair is an explosive form of energy. They asked you, "How can we save ourselves?" You spoke to them about the rights of others, but they became impatient and would say decisively, "We have no choice but to fight. There is no other way out. We won't die without fighting. Death on the battlefield is better than death at home." Feelings of a suicidal Masada exploded inside them. And they drank voraciously as though they were drinking life itself. The lover made up with his sweetheart, and the virgins became mothers at an amazing speed. The divorced man returned to his wife. Opposing political parties formed a coalition, and a national front came into being. And they searched for a national hero.

They said goodbye, and did not come back.[21]

IV

When you walk the streets of the city, you feel alone. It is not the color of your skin that declares your identity, or being chased by the police. The street itself is damning you, declaring who you are because you are the only young man around. Whoever walked in the street at that time was an Arab. The old people and the young damn you, and you become ashamed of being in the street. All the falafel and sandwich stands are empty, and all the cinemas. The entire country is empty of young people. There are many newspapers around. You do not know who delivers or reads them. But you notice that it is the elementary school kids who deliver the mail and the milk bottles.

They taught you to be wary of happiness because it hurts when it betrays. So from where did it come so suddenly?

Your waiting approaches the point of explosion. Your mother asks you to be careful. Destiny – your destiny – can take the shape of a bullet. You see the war, but you do not see your death. Memories come rushing out of you all at once. There is no time to imagine what lies ahead. Suddenly, you remember that Palestine is your country. The lost name leads you to lost ages. It seems as if this lady sleeping on the coast of the Mediterranean is jolted awake when you call her by her enthralling name. They denied you your old school songs and the stories of the revolutionaries and poets who sang her praises. The name returns. At last it returns from its trip to the absurd. You open its map as if undoing the buttons of your first lover for the first time. Everything looks silver. Tiberias comes into view. You go up to Jerusalem as if mounting to the waist of a god. Safad jumps out for the first kiss. In Acre love makes you sit on the rocks by the seashore. You look at the map and whistle a happy, merry tune. You forget Haifa because you always forget your heart. You feel a deep friendship with the days. They were not as harsh as you had imagined, but their jesting was sometimes hideous. What a world! You feel with your long fingers the parts of the sweet-smelling woman lying on polished leaves: the waist is narrow, licked by the sea and the boundary of the truce. Then you kiss her and hug her and die of the pleasure and the promise. You are not on earth but lost, lost and fascinated by ambiguity. You remember your difficult childhood and the future's childhood and that of the trees. Then you cross the streets of Acre and pause on the Beirut road. You had the feeling of a miracle when your older friends told you about their weekly trips to Damascus, Beirut, and Cairo. Take the train from Haifa; it passes by al-Arish before it drops you in Cairo. Or take a taxi from Acre and in less than one hour you will be at al-Burj Square in Beirut, and will finish your evening of pleasure by the River Barada in Damascus, which you imagine to be the size of your happiness. You ask your friends, "Are Beirut, Cairo, and Damascus so close?" They were. They were even closer. Palestine was the meeting point of the East. Abdul Wahhab sang here, and so did Umm Kulthum. If you stood by the Pyramids and hurled a stone at Palestine, it would arrive as a bird. And now what? A bird leaves Palestine and lays eggs that hatch a flock of refugees at the outskirts of Damascus. They tore us to pieces, and we multiplied as refugees, some on the outside and some on the inside. On the outside the children grow up on the milk of the United Nations Relief and Works Agency, and in their veins it becomes Palestinian blood. And on the inside, you eat the wheat of Marj Ibn Amer, and you become a "citizen of Israel." You spend half your life looking for a single acknowledgment that you are a Palestinian citizen, and you do not find one. And on the very day that a human being landed on the moon, you were busy writing an emotional letter to the Israeli police appealing for permission to travel to the village where your people live. On the outside they envy you because you are still in your homeland while they are refugees. You tell them that the mere sight of water does not satisfy the thirsty man but bloodies him. Nothing separates you from your land except a street. If you crossed it, you would be arrested and accused of infiltration and damaging state property. Better stand on the sidewalk and turn into a dried-up tree. Between you and death there is only the edge of a knife. When you see them plowing your land the plow cuts into your heart. And when you cry out with pain and frustration, they accuse you of anti-Semitism.

This is poetry, and the river is not near. You prefer poetry to crossing rivers, but bloated critics take you to task for confessions you did not make and did not choose, and that have nothing to do with you. An outright denial would mean a public rejection. This way the equation becomes deadly: to reject my enemies in this manner means to reject my existence. You have to be crafty with the formulation in order to safeguard your existence. For this reason you prefer poetry to crossing rivers. Then critics living in ease will accuse you of being a traitor to the national cause. And your enemies will accuse you of anti-Semitism.

Stand on the sidewalk and turn into a dried-up tree. When you see them satisfying the thirst of the earth with water, the joy sent by rain flows in abundance. The important thing is that the land should not remain thirsty, even if you yourself die of thirst. That is what your grandfather used to do. He spent the remainder of his life standing on the sidewalk next to the edge of the knife. And between his transformation into a dried-up tree, his joy at the falling rain, and the plunge of the plow into his heart, it stopped and he died. Your brother who loves to write gave his funeral oration, promising that the next funeral will be accompanied by better fortune than this one:

"You buried your grandfather – the tree that dried up – in the ground, and now he is in a grave he did not wish for. The living are deprived of their homes and their land, and the dead are deprived of their graves."

You no longer went down to the street in those days. You sat in your room and shook the dust from the names of your cities. Palestine discovered its name, and love returned.

V

Everything started.

And everything ended.

Between the beginning and the ending, the happiness that you were always wary of betrayed you. All was transformed from stones into thoughts. In the shelter you were hanging on the tightrope between two days that did not resemble each other. Let the homeland be silent for a moment. Enmity has now struck between you and life itself. The earthquake shook you, and you fell to the ground. They have returned to Jerusalem – the general, the rabbi, and the harlot. "We will never leave." They beat their heads against the stones of the old wall until their blood flowed. No war without blood. They did not lose much blood in this war, and now they declare the price of the war in the blood given with free will to the stones of the temple. You hear them speaking on the radio. They have reached the Lord over the corpses of your people who did not defend themselves. Violence yet again: violence has proven its worth. Just claims will not grant you anything or allow you to keep anything. You do not usually weep easily, but the fall of

Jerusalem means falling tears. Their prayers awaken you. When after two days you lift the curtain of the shelter an avalanche of light overwhelms you, coming from a Haifa that had been entrenched in a sham blackout. Before this day you never saw a people capable of such savage joy. The drums beat, children's whistles sounded, and lights flared. They did not rejoice at the fall of Jerusalem, the West Bank, Sinai, and the Golan Heights as they are now rejoicing. Gamal Abdel Nasser has fallen. The symbol, the voice, and the hope. A small item of news the size of death. Three young men in Nazareth had heart attacks and died. The villages of Upper Egypt and the other regions are advancing on Cairo to bring Nasser back to the helm. How can a symbol be the size of the homeland? Because the survival of the symbol gives rise to hopes of regaining the homeland. When Abdel Nasser said, "Citizens and brothers!" and started speaking, everything came to a standstill. The hungry became full, and the expatriate came home. And Palestine stood on its feet waiting to be liberated. When Abdel Nasser said, "Citizens and brothers!" and started speaking, the inhabitants of the Occupied Territories from the youngest to the oldest locked themselves to the radio. They would often rush to the apparatus that carried the voice of Abdel Nasser and kiss it with an indescribable feeling of human and national exultation. And now he is gone! Our devotion to liberation and the home-land was tied to Nasser's return. When he did come back, the Arabs felt they had achieved victory, snatching hope from the clutches of defeat.

You leave the newspaper drafts in the shelter. What did you write? You covered news of the battles, wrote the text, arranged the columns, and corrected the proofs because your colleagues in the editing department had been arrested. Some policemen came early that Monday morning and called out the name of a colleague. They put his wrists in iron and led him in sight of everyone to the police car. Then they came back and called out another name until no one was left in the office except you and the editor in chief. The paper was scheduled to come out the next morning on time. It was important for it to come out to provide a ray of hope to readers who had nothing to protect them against psychological warfare except you and your colleagues. The editor then turned to you and said, "Take your papers and go somewhere else. It's your turn next." You went somewhere to continue your writing. Later you learned that your colleagues had been led like captives to the city square in plain view of the Israeli public, which had its view of war prisoners. Who was responsible for the decision to arrest people inside the country? On June fourth the chief of staff signed the list containing the names of those chosen for arrest. Everything is organized. In your hideout you do not know the truth. The Arabs announce they had entered Palestine, and the Israelis do not deny anything. You can hear the terror that had overcome everyone outside the apartment. And you hear that the police had run amok in the expectant Arab villages in the area. Curses, beatings, and torture. Yet the people count these as their last moments of bondage, for this war was to be the last gasp of the [Israeli] swan. The radio tells you that the petrol refinery had been burning for hours, and you note this item of news. But in a short while you remember that your hideout overlooks the port. You part the screen to steal a glance at the refineries, and you see no fire. The fire is in the heart. Then an item of news arrives from the Israeli parliament. They have been raising their glasses from the first hours of the battle. Are they crazy? Celebrating! How can this be? They say they have abolished the legend of Abdel Nasser's army. At midnight, the army chief of staff announces on the radio the fruit of the battles: the Egyptian air force was destroyed at dawn, and the Israeli forces are already on the outskirts of Rafah.

And you return – you return from your too short journey into hope back to Haifa. You return to the truth. Who is going to tell you the truth? The enemy? My people promised they would come, and I waited. They set off, and I waited full of hope. Patriotic songs, radio stations, and coups d'état have transported me to fields I used to dream of. They took me toward my humanity, and abandoned me halfway there. O Arabs, why are you lying to me? You did not put these passing thoughts in the newspaper. You wrote about other things. Even Abdel Nasser has now gone away and left me to myself, with no homeland, and no Nasser as well.

That is how everything began.

And that is how everything ended.

—Where have you been?

—Here, at home.

—Why haven't you opened the door for six days?

—Because I don't receive visitors in wartime.

—And why did you open now?

—Because prison is preferable to staying at home. And because I canceled all my appointments. I'm ready for arrest. Ready. Take me.

Then came a captain, a sergeant, and a policeman.

As you descended the stairs to the police car, you said goodbye to the house and the eyes of the neighbors hidden behind the windows, but you did not feel you were saying goodbye to freedom. You always believed that the police van was taking you to your true freedom. You like to call things by their real names, and this is the real name of prison. In prison you do not say, "Everything has ended." You say, "Everything has just begun, and the beginning is freedom."

Everything has just begun.

Your colleagues in the prison pounce, wanting to squeeze a different kind of news out of you. They have no access to the news except the broadcasts of the enemy, and they do not believe any of it. All they want is just one item of news, but you have none to offer. "My friends," I say, "I'm sorry to tell you that what you heard is the truth." Some of them feel angry and their eyes accuse you of despair before they walk away. Prison is just fine. You have always been waiting for something to happen, and you busy yourself with looking after small needs. One hour a day you see the sun, and that brings you back to your vanquished friendship with life. One little patch of blue brings joy to your heart, and when you get out you will eat up the whole earth. In prison all became expert in military matters, and we found just one cause for the defeat: treason. Anyone who dared doubt that was accused of being deviant.

Yet, how will everything begin, and where will it lead you? Either your feeling of being "an Arab citizen in Israel" will deepen, or your rejection of this identity – of which you had no choice – will deepen. The first choice would be a reaction to the dashed hope that the Arabs have inflicted upon you, and a strengthening of your resolve to carry on with the modest political action possible within the compass of Israeli law: "Everything depends on the inside, and all demands for democracy must be based on acceptance of the fait accompli." The second choice would be a response to the Israeli violence you invite when you practice the identity of your choice: "Everything depends on the outside, and without an Israeli military defeat no essential change can take place in Israeli society."

There is a difference between the two options, but not a huge contradiction in their consequences as far as your actions in the present circumstances are concerned, as long as you exist on the inside and the outside at once.

The outside option has been decisively defeated, but not the sense of your identification with it. This identity is not a mere point of view or an opinion subject to debate. It is a historical fact. Yet, suddenly, you register a moral contradiction. The most you can achieve in your struggle from within can only be done under the banner of an "Israeli nationality" that is in contradiction to a national identity with roots in history. Hence, you start to shake violently and breathe heavily. You do not need to look for reassurance because reassurance is not the issue. You can say, for example, that the condition in which you find yourself is not of your own making. You can also say that there lies the contradiction, but it is not a pressing political problem now. One day, however, the contradiction will crumble, and the waiting will turn into a psychological complex. When that happens living in harmony with self will be difficult to achieve.

But you leave the question hanging, for poetry is your form of expression and poetic language avoids murderous questions. Poetry has something to say, and it has nothing to say. Poetry speaks truth, but does not announce it. This is your homeland, and the response to the conquerors enhances your love for it because any weak point in the relationship between you and it is an opening for them. They put Palestine in the pockets of their military uniforms, yet Palestine remains your homeland, be it a map, a massacre, a land, or an idea. It is your homeland indeed. No dagger will convince you it belongs to them. Your acceptance of the challenge and of this prison protects you from a change of heart. Thanks to the prison warden for making you one with freedom. Thanks to the shackles for reminding your arms they cannot hug a tree. You write to your imaginary lover: "I wish despair for you, my love, that you may excel, for the desperate are creative. Don't wait for me. Don't wait for anyone. Wait for the thought; don't wait for the thinker. Wait for the poem; don't wait for the poet. Wait for the revolution; don't wait for the revolutionary. The thinker may be wrong, the poet may lie, and the revolutionary may get tired. This is the despair I mean."

You did not embrace any shadows; therefore you have nothing to regret.

The happiness that came upon you suddenly – that was the arrival of the unexpected. The defeat was a harsh betrayal. Very well. You will carry on with your work, with your feeling of being torn apart, and your ambivalence. And before everything else, you will carry on with your refusal. You will not say yes to anything. You emerged from the happiness with a defeat, and you emerged from the defeat with a new refusal, not only of the enemy. Has your homeland become only an idea? Hang on to the idea, then. The road from Haifa to Tel Aviv is the true aesthetic miracle. The Mediterranean to your right, and the chain of mountains to your left, and the chains of iron on your wrists. The homeland is at its most beautiful when it is on the other side of the barbed wire.

In court the law achieves parity with the gun. The law will not stand with you as long as your gun is down. In various ways the killers always talk of morality. Some soldiers "regret" getting rid of prisoners by killing them, but they will say there was no alternative. An old friend comes to visit you, her hands filled with almonds from the West Bank. They no longer feel fear; they are no longer Jews. In Acre you see Egyptian prisoners, and you feel a shock. They came to liberate you, and became prisoners instead. The Arabs for whom you have been waiting also arrive. The refugees return: they come back as tourists and prisoners. The Arabic nationalist songs are now muffled, the sound of Hebrew national songs is now louder, and the Israeli has become a legend. And Palestine sleeps on the shores of distant rivers. It does not bathe in water but in the blood of the future. Will there be a new birth? This is how it should be. There will have to be a birth. Will death hone us into shape? That is how it should be. We must also be honed by happiness. The resistance will begin. The resistance will begin. Everything has come to an end, and the resistance will begin. And if happiness should surprise you again, do not mention its previous betrayal.

Enter into the happiness, and burst.

Improvisations on the Sura of Jerusalem [22]

❧

Today was hung on a piece of wood, she who has kept us hanging with longing.[23]

Today you are all crying over Jerusalem, and Jerusalem does not cry for anyone.[24]

When tears are tied to the hands of the clock, Jerusalem becomes time, and the place our eyes. Everything is outside us – the cities, the tears, the evening that does not end. Inside us the guns aimed at aircraft and the longing of the Prophets settle into position. We have called Jerusalem by all the names that are not suitable for her, and we declared our worthiness of it by means not suitable for us – painting, poetry, the Security Council, treason, and death. We have not produced a single Jeremiah who can walk around in our streets and our failings, one who can put curses on us and write our lamentations.

If the curse does not pursue us, we will never come to our senses.

And if lamentations do not reach us, we will never know the taste of gladness.

Let them stop. Let the tears of today that resemble the tears of yesterday stop.

Let us search for another color for tomorrow's tears, for we have no wall to receive them. Jerusalem is the capital of faraway tents, faraway capital, and faraway martyrs. Let them stop. Let the tears of today stop until Jerusalem becomes the capital of the color red sculpted from the waters of the River Jordan.

I entered it shielded by courage, afraid of courage.

It happened only once in my life, to see history armed with all these weapons and ferocious olive branches. It never happened that a human turned into a rock, and it never happened that a rock turned into a soldier.

Yet that happened in Jerusalem. I was the rock and the human being and the soldier.

As of now, this moment, Paradise is nearer. I will exchange Paradise for Jerusalem because Paradise is not so beautiful or disgraced, and because it is a promise that has not yet proven to be false.

Who taught me this silence, and who taught Jerusalem to keep time with an evening that has no end?

Who taught me all this courage? And who taught Jerusalem all this irony?

No. Homeland is not like the bond between shade and tree or blade and sheath. Homeland is not a relationship of blood and kinship. And homeland is not a religion or a god. Homeland is this alienation. This alienation. This alienation that preys upon you in Jerusalem.

As a result of this, Paradise is nearer.

It was not a meeting or a farewell.

The moment that separates meeting from farewell, or flesh from bone – this is where you are when you meet Jerusalem.

You descend upon the newspaper vendors, the remainders of ruins, and the sellers of falafel and fresh vegetables and imported canned goods who have all learned the language of the conquerors overnight. You descend upon them with the frenzy of suicide. You grab their things and shout in the loudest silence: "Who will buy a historic breast, a historic back, and historic genitals in a single moment of victory?" Then you smile for the conquerors.

Your back bends like an Arab bow when the Arabs were knights before they knew petrol and national radio stations, and you prepare for an obscure action. In the beginning was the action, or was it the word? You hesitate.

Would that your back were made of metal, that it may not crack.

Would that your silence were made of metal, that it may sound or ring out.

Then a dream transports you to the gates of the city: Who in a moment of victory will buy your history as an ornament? An ornament. You are the prince of believers that resistance is a right, and death is a right.

Jerusalem never belonged to me. I am the newspaper vendor in every age and language. Those who are the owners of Jerusalem sell me out and receive the conquerors, and speak of culture and anthropology. Jerusalem never belonged to me. Give me other newspapers and other news because I do not know how to read.

(That's what the newspaper vendor said.)

—Its windows do not look out on anything.

It is open. The countless hills come to it during the days of war. In the days of war, only the dead are counted. The hills and the sun arrive, and the guns of the conquerors on which "Jerusalem the Golden" is inscribed.[25]

Within the compass of a small dream, I saw myself emerging from the cell on Mount Carmel that shielded me from the shape of the war. Did anyone see me in Jerusalem that I may apologize to him? I will not go back there because its windows do not look out on anything that concerns me.

A young soldier stopped me and asked about my hand grenade and my prayer. "I don't fight," I said to her, hiding a sense of shame, "and I don't pray."

"Why did you come to Jerusalem then?" she asked.

"To pass between the gun and the prayer: to my right the ruins of a war, and to my left the ruins of a god. But I don't fight and I don't pray."

"What are you, then?" asked the soldier.

"A lottery ticket between the grenade and the prayer."

"What will you do with it, and what will it do with you if you should win?"

"I will buy a color for the eyes of my lover."

The soldier believed I was a poet, and let me go.

"Why did I come to Jerusalem, then?" I asked myself.

(The speaker: Mahmoud Darwish)

A treasure made of rocks, defeat, and rare trees.

If my city were with me now, I would relinquish my throat and drink the ice-cold water of a spring that lives in a mountain.

If my city were with me now, I would send apologies for all my appointments (even the ones I made with death), which I usually keep, arriving five minutes early.

A box made of rock, a great amount of sun, and an inspiring defeat.

In the beginning was not the action, or the word; in the beginning was the defeat.

If my city were in my luggage now, I would have departed. He who saw me would consider me an enemy and kill me because my city is beautiful, like a love not yet born. Evening is always slow and orange in color.

A painting made of rock, hanging on seven hills, three thousand years, fifty prophets, four million daggers, a tree, five United Nations resolutions, and a million or more dead.

I offer her my hand, but it does not reach her.

One day I arrived before my hand, and stumbled over a number. I did not take hold of anything, because I arrived before my hand, and my heart would not leave my chest.

The numbers flow copiously in blood and eyes and dates and shoes and laments and thrones and nails and poems. The numbers flow out and kill me, raising the count of the dead, the lovers, and the names of Jerusalem. And evening is always slow and orange in color. Gentlemen, I was lying. Jerusalem is not this city. This city is not Jerusalem.

(Thus spoke an emotional young lady working for the Department of Tourism.)

Silence for the Sake of Gaza

❧

She wraps explosives around her waist and blows herself up.

It is not a death, and not a suicide.

It is Gaza's way of declaring she is worthy of life.

For four years Gaza's flesh has been torn into shrapnel flying in all directions.

It is not magic, and it is not a miracle.

It is Gaza's weapon for defending herself and exhausting the enemy.

For four years the enemy had been delighted with his dreams, fascinated by his dalliance with time, except in Gaza because Gaza is far from her kin and sits right up against the enemy. Because Gaza is an island: every time she erupts – and she is always erupting – she lacerates the face of the enemy, breaks up his dreams, and obstructs his contentment with time. Because time in Gaza is something else: time in Gaza is not a neutral element. Gaza does not propel people to cool contemplation; rather she propels them to erupt and collide with the truth. Time there does not lead children directly from childhood to old age, but it does make men of them upon the first encounter with the enemy. Time in Gaza does not allow you to let go; rather it is an attack upon a blistering noon because values in Gaza are different. Different. Different. The only values that an occupied person can espouse are those of resistance to occupation. This is the only competition there. Familiarity with these noble and hard values has become a need in Gaza. Her people did not acquire this need from books, or from brief academic courses, or from trumpets blaring propaganda, or from patriotic songs. Only from experience did Gaza learn these values, and from actions not performed for the sake of one's image or self-promotion.

Gaza does not show off her weapons, her revolutionary zeal, or her balance sheet. She offers her bitter flesh, follows her own will, and pours out her blood.

Gaza has not mastered the orator's art. Gaza does not have a throat. The pores of her skin speak in sweat, blood, and fire.

As a result the enemy hates her enough to kill, is afraid enough to commit crimes, and tries to sink her in the sea, in the desert, or in blood.

Therefore her friends and relations love her with a feeling of shame that touches on jealousy, or even fear sometimes, because Gaza is the savage lesson and radiant model for enemies and friends alike.

Gaza is not the most beautiful of cities.

Her coast is not bluer than those of other Arab cities.

Her oranges are not the best in the Mediterranean.

Gaza is not the richest of cities.

(Fish and oranges and sand and tents forsaken by the winds, smuggled goods, and hands for hire.)

And Gaza is not the most polished of cities, or the largest. But she is equivalent to the history of a nation, because she is the most repulsive among us in the eyes of the enemy – the poorest, the most desperate, and the most ferocious. Because she is a nightmare. Because she is oranges that explode, children without a childhood, aged men without an old age, and women without desire. Because she is all that, she is the most beautiful among us, the purest, the richest, and most worthy of love.

We are unfair to her when we search for her poems. Let us not disfigure the beauty of Gaza. The most beautiful thing in her is that she is free of poetry at a time when the rest of us tried to gain victory with poems. We believed ourselves and rejoiced when we saw that the enemy had left us alone to sing our songs while we left victory for him. When we dried the poems from our lips we saw that the enemy had already built entire cities, forts, and highways.

It would be unfair to turn Gaza into a legend because we will end up hating her when we discover she is nothing more than a small, poor city that resists. And when we ask, "What has made her into a legend?" we will have to break our mirrors and cry if we have any dignity, or curse her if we refused to rebel against ourselves.

It would be unfair to Gaza to glorify her because our fascination will make us wait for her. But Gaza will not come to us. Gaza will not liberate us. Gaza does not have horses, or jet fighters, or magic wands, or offices in capitals. Gaza frees herself of our attributes, our language, and of her conquerors all at once. And when we run into her, once upon a dream, she may not recognize us because she was born of fire while we were born of waiting and crying over our homes.

True, Gaza has her special circumstances and her own revolutionary traditions.

(We say this not to dissect but to disintegrate.)

The secret of Gaza is no mystery: her masses are united in popular resistance. She knows what she wants: to drive the enemy out of her hair. In Gaza the relation between resistance and the masses is that of the flesh to the bone, and not that of the teacher to the student.

In Gaza resistance has not become a salaried position.

And in Gaza resistance has not become an institution.

She does not accept supervision from anyone, and she does not allow her destiny to hang on anyone's stamp or signature.

It does not matter to her very much whether or not we know her name, or recognize her image or oratorical skills. She does not believe she is photogenic or a media event. She does not make ready for the camera with a smile plastered on her face.

That is not what she wants, and not what we want.

Gaza's wound has not been changed into a platform for orators. What is beautiful about Gaza is that we do not discuss her much, and we do not perfume the smoke of her dreams with the feminine fragrance of our lyrics.

Thus, Gaza would make a losing bet for the bookies. And for this very reason Gaza is a moral and spiritual treasure of incalculable worth for all Arabs.

What is beautiful about Gaza is that our voices do not reach her. Nothing diverts her attention. Nothing turns her fist away from the face of the enemy: not the kind of Palestinian state that we will establish on the eastern side of the moon, or the western side of Jupiter after it has been mapped, or the distribution of seats in the [Palestine] National Council. Nothing diverts her attention. She is dedicated to rejection. Hunger and rejection. Thirst and rejection. Dispersion and rejection. Torture and rejection. Siege and rejection. Death and rejection.

The enemy may defeat Gaza. (The stormy sea might overwhelm a small island.)

They might cut down all her trees.

They might break her bones.

They might plant their tanks in the bellies of her women and children, or they might toss her into the sand, into the sea, into blood.

But:

Gaza will not repeat the lies.

Gaza will not say yes to the conquerors.

And she will continue to erupt.

It is not death, and it is not suicide, it is Gaza's way of announcing she is worthy of life.

Going to the World

❧

A Stranger in the World

At a dark hour of the night the world repairs to the bedroom.

Its day was full. Tranquillity engulfed the earth. The trappings of Western civilization still wrestled with human will in Asia. The soil of Asia was dying, the people of Asia were dying, and the rivers swept away those who missed their encounter with the trappings of civilization. Close to the Mediterranean Sea, military boots made in the West still trampled down the old culture and the new human being. In ordinary, very ordinary, news bulletins whole fields of children were mowed down because they were Arabs and had the power to grow up.

At a late hour of the morning the world rises and leaves the bedroom for the operations room. Its night was clear, with nonstop dreams of happiness.

In this manner the world sleeps.

In this manner the world wakes from its sleep.

And in this manner it forgets all about me.

It does not remember me except when I seek death or when I seek life.

Today, today the world did not repair to the bedroom. It stood at the edge of the earth and ordered me to exit from the circle of humanity because I tried to penetrate the circle. I tried to enter.

—World, what have you to do with my history?

—History is the past, and I study it in school.

—Where did you see me for the first time?

—I always saw you on the soil of Palestine until you left, then peace and tranquillity returned to the earth. Why are you returning now? Why do you disturb our peace of mind?

This is how the world understands me, and this is how it wants me to be. Our conflict is over as long as I have left Palestine, and there is no one to guard the fire. The equation of peace on earth is complete, and international security becomes conditional upon my absence from Palestine, and from humanity.

I did not say goodbye to anyone or anything. The butt of a rifle rolled me down from Mount Carmel to the port of Haifa. I was clinging to God's waste and crying at the top of my voice until I lost my voice and my mind. But the world promised me some alms in exchange for signing a truce with myself (because a truce with the killer cannot be accomplished without a truce with oneself first). And the world did give alms: it gave flour, clothes, and many tents for me and my children, who were not born in exchange for homeland and peace. When I felt cold in my exile, newspapers of world public opinion protected me from the rains and from shivering with cold. When I felt hungry, three lines in the speech of the head of a civilized nation satisfied my hunger. And when I felt longing, the foreign songs blaring out of the neighbors' radio turned departure into a lovely experience.

This is how the world goes to its bedroom and forgets me.

—Do not wake up the victim! He might cry out!

—Who woke him? Who is responsible?

—A wind that blew unexpectedly, waking the dead.

—From what direction did it blow?

—From all directions. From the homeland.

—Who taught them this forgotten word?

—Poets singing to the tunes of a rebec.

—Kill them!

—We killed them, but they came up with a new word: freedom.

—Who taught them this rebellious word?

—Impassioned revolutionaries.

—Kill them!

—We killed them, but they learned a new word: justice.

—Who taught them this word?

—Oppression. Shall we kill oppression?

—If you do away with oppression, then you will be doing away with yourselves.

—What shall we do?

—Kill the memory.

This is how the world goes to sleep, and in the same way it wakes up. It is armed with weapons to the hilt, and we are armed to the hilt with shackles. The powerful are civilized, and the weak are savage. History is not a judge. History is a functionary. What would the Red Indians have said if they had defeated their conquerors? Those who boast of being cultured and civilized are most often the killers. The killers. Consider this threesome. The first annihilated a people in the past. They have detonated the great sign of their civilization – the atom bomb – in the streets of the world, and are now annihilating a people and a land in Southeast Asia. They are demanding that I exit from the human race and the globe because I am a terrorist. As for the second, it is best not to remind them of their past. They have burned tens of millions of people in the name of culture and civilization. And now, the killer and the victim embrace and give birth to a new offspring, who is the third. What can come out of the marriage of terrorist with terrorist except terrorism? The third, armed to the hilt with the Hebrew Bible and the sword, came and uprooted me from my hills and valleys and rolled me out of civilization down into the depths. This threesome is now demanding I exit from the earth because I am a terrorist.

And what was the world doing?

At a late hour of the night it went to its bedroom and fell asleep.

Murder is always a crime. So, why should killing become one of the pillars of the temple of civilization when practiced by the powerful?

Was Israel established by any other means than killing and terrorism? Such is the world, always: most admiring of collective killing and most critical of individual killing. The state has a right to kill its own people and those belonging to other nations, but the individual does not have a right to fight for the sake of freedom.

Who is this "world public opinion"?

When we ask for justice from killers, then "world public opinion" must be understood metaphorically as long as the expression refers to media owned by individuals whose ideology and interests are linked. Why then should we accord it all this reverence? As for the true public opinion – human conscience – we do not see it or hear its voice because the official institution of "world public opinion" in the West has stifled and falsified it. If our actions are subject to the requirements of "world public opinion" as expressed in the official media, then it is time for us to realize that we enjoy our bondage and our loss, and should start looking for reasons to prolong them. When this "public opinion" is the property of individuals, are they then worthy of being the judges? When we shun suicide, they say we are cowards. And when we embrace it, they say we are barbarians. When we call for peace, they say we are lying hypocrites. And when we prepare for battle, they say we are savages. But are we the killers? Who killed whom? Did they ask this question?

It is not true that the world has lost its memory. And it is also not true that we can make the world remember by pleasing it. The world wants to relax. It wants to gamble and sip whiskey.

—Why are you waking the world from its slumber?

—What you hear is not my voice. It's the sound of my corpse hitting the ground.

—Why don't you die quietly then?

—Because a quiet death is a degrading life.

—And a loud death?

—It is to stand firm.

—Did you come to announce your presence?

—No. I came to announce my absence.

—Why do you kill, then?

—I don't kill anything except killing. I kill only the crime.

—Go to hell!

—I am coming from hell.

For the first time, the world asked itself, "Who told him he's a bomb?"

—They shot him with so many bullets that shrapnel piled upon shrapnel and generated enough energy for him to turn into an explosive device.

—Push him out of the sphere of the world.

—We pushed him out but he came back.

—Set up an ambush for him at the edge of the earth, and push him into the vacuum.

—You can't get close to him because he is armed to the teeth with a quarter century of tragedy, anger, and volatility.

—A terrorist?

—Yes. A terrorist, and desperate.

What do they do with despair? Despair is the twin brother of death. I want nothing from the world except to move the knife away from my throat. I was a hostage. I have been your hostage for twenty-five years, and despair released me. What will bring hope back except the declaration of my despair? And what will release me from bondage except my ability to kill myself? Let the world go to its bedroom. I am a safety valve for the world. This is the role that you have defined for me, and it is not up to you to determine the form of my objection to gratuitous death. You cannot determine the method I choose to save myself from perpetual slaughter. If there is nothing for me but death, then I will die the way I want. I am not content with this role. I am not content. My enslavement should not be equivalent to your security. Call me what you want. Now it is my turn to call myself what I want, and do what I want to do. I will plant my foot in the heart of the world. I will tear my arm out and wave it in the air. I will turn it into a ball and play with you. I will throw it into your nets, O judges of civilization. Not for the sake of the homeland. Not for the sake of the people. And not for revenge. This is the way it suits me, as an Asian beast, to use my body. I will train it to move, after a paralysis that has lasted a quarter of a century. I will cut it into pieces in order to amuse you. This is my only freedom. Why then do you object to my killing myself, O experts in collective killing? You who transform children into charcoal. You kill, therefore you live. And I kill myself, therefore I live. As of now, I will allow no one to kill me except myself. Do you know who I am? UNRWA milk does not turn into milk in the veins, it turns into dynamite. This is what you dish out coming back to you. When my mother threw me into your streets you kicked me out and said, "Go back to your mother." When I came back to my mother, you arrested me, tortured me, and called me a terrorist. And from that moment, I have been searching for my mother. Do you know where I found her? My body was oozing blood, and when I awoke from my coma I found myself in a pool of blood. I looked closely and saw features that I called my mother's face. That was my blood, not yours, O judges of the world!

He who made me into a refugee transformed me into a bomb. I know I will die, and I know that today I am waging a losing battle because it is the battle of tomorrow. I know that Palestine – on the map – is far from where I am. And I know that you have forgotten her name, and now use a new translation of that name. I know all this, and that is why I carry her into your streets, your houses, and your bedrooms.

Going to the Arabic Sentence on May 15

࿔

I

May finds you sitting between anemones and the gun.

This is the beginning of the exodus, and the end of the earth. To everything there is a season except your death. Like tropical rain it will come suddenly and repeatedly on no special occasion. Where then will you find a moment for a proper celebration of the first death? You are defeated from jugular to jugular. And there you are, passing between the sound and its echo, a new Christ without a liturgy. In the Arabic sentence there is enough room for a continent of tents. Settle into one of them and dream of a cooler hot summer.

May finds you sitting between anemones and the gun.

Homeland is not an ancient rock, even if it were warm like a body. How naïve you would be to put yourself and your fire under siege with such a limited and primitive dream: the absolute homeland! Do not ask who gave the earth this narrow expanse. From the Gulf to the Ocean, there are thousands of hearts that will give you support and shelter. Go to the Arabic sentence, and you will find self and homeland. Yet in time there will be room for war and peace.

May finds you sitting between anemones and the gun.

What would you do if you were to get out of this role? This way of being has provided you with food and drink. They throw money and donations at your wounds. Where would you find your food if the wounds were to heal? All those who discovered freedom before you swore at it and longed for the days when they were searching for it. What is a state but a police force and taxes? Are you spilling all this blood merely for the sake of policing and new taxes? The glory of Christ is that he was crucified at the height of his mission. Imagine. Imagine what would have happened to the world if Christ had come down from the cross. Chaos and apostasy. The priests, the artists, and the poor would have rebelled against him. They would have forced him back to his wounds, barefoot or with new shoes so that others may carry on with their lives. Go to the Arabic sentence: savor the surge of support and dream of the well-being of the Arabic language. Many conquerors have passed through. (Have other peoples had the same experience with conquerors as we have had?) They occupied the land and dispersed the people, but they never could penetrate the barrier of a single guttural sound of the language.

May finds you between anemones and the gun.

O my native land! I know the way to you, but I do not know you. For a quarter of a century I've been returning to you by way of the Arabic sentence, and have been a stranger to both. I am a stranger to you, and to it also. They liked the anemones, and tried to steal my gun. I fired in the air, and hit the anemones. They accused me of attempted suicide and took me to court. Shall I keep quiet to come closer to you, or defend you and myself with the Arabic sentence?

II

The birthday party came to an end. The Holy City does not have an organized memory. The sky was pouring with rain and conquerors. The new soldier was having a good time with his old girlfriend in the quarters of the conquered city. "If I forget you, sweetheart," he was saying, "may my arm forget me!" He forgot his arm in her bosom, and she accused him of betraying her, "Do you love Jerusalem more than me?" They laughed and carried on with their merriment. They recalled memories of the 1967 War and wondered how it was possible to live without Jerusalem. He invented stories of his heroism in action.

They bought falafel from an Arab vendor who had learned to speak Hebrew with a Polish accent.

"They have grown used to us. Did you know that time is an officer in the Israeli army who gets a promotion every year?" She took off her shoes and walked barefoot. "Do you want me to prove that to you?" He bought a newspaper from an Arab vendor who was hawking the new edition of *al-Masa'* in excellent Hebrew.

"Arabic coffee has a heady taste. What will our life be like without these people? Do you imagine we could maintain our national unity if we had to live without them?"

They entered the Dome of the Rock compound, and exchanged a kiss within view of the myth. "Let legend bear witness that the people of Israel are alive!" They felt sorry because they had exchanged a kiss there previously for remembrance, with the feeling of tourists who would not be coming back. And here they were, coming back every year. "This kiss is not just for remembrance, but to arouse the legend."

It was raining. It always rains on Christmas Day. It pleased him to compare the natural qualities of his urine with the rain. He found a hidden corner, and then came back to tell her about a slight difference in color. "The Arabs have some praiseworthy traits, like generosity and the ability to forget." She answered without paying attention, "I don't like them." He came back with another argument, "If it weren't for them, we wouldn't have met and I wouldn't have fallen in love with you. And for our love to continue and be fruitful, there must be Arabs." They recalled their old differences when they were studying in the Faculty of Letters, but the evening tempted them to embrace again. He kissed her, and continued, "They are the essence of our unity. I am from Warsaw, and you are from Baghdad. What makes the Jew a Jew is the challenge, and his need to hold himself together. What is the mainstay of our holding together? The Arabs are our shared challenge. If they disappear, so will our unity, and the challenge would be transferred to the relation between the one who comes from Warsaw and the one who comes from Baghdad." She reminded him he had to get to sleep early that night in order to feel awake and strong for the military parade the next day.

At that moment, the street cleaners were sweeping away the debris from a week of religious celebration. Christ was in retreat, and the Holy City was in the process of betraying her memory and opening her streets for the celebrations of the new conquerors, who were singing "Jerusalem the Golden."

At that moment also, they were receiving unexpected presents and greeting cards: Arab blood was flowing in the streets of Beirut, and was turning into oil that satisfied the thirst of the ancient cedars presented to King Solomon for building the Temple.

III

Who will bring an end to dispersion?

A few days ago we were asking, who will bring an end to the defeat, and now we are shouting, who will bring an end to dispersion and the forced expulsion of this woman?

The same picture always appears after the bullets: a Palestinian mother, dragging her children along, lugging her bedding, and walking into the wind and the unknown. She goes from one place of refuge to another. When will she settle down in a final refuge before death? It seems that the call for the return has been postponed. For a quarter of a century we have seen it walking on our bones (Who are we to speak in this manner? – observers). She leaves one refugee camp in the direction of another tent, or a leaning rock, pursued by curses, shells, and destinies set down on paper. Call her what you will, for she is my mother.

—Set up for her a tent made of cement, so that she may stop running. Let her settle down in one shelter.

—The bedding carried on the head and the homeland carried in the heart are held together by a single thread. If the bedding were to find a resting place, the homeland would be lost.

—Has being a refugee now become a poster and an ornament?

The dialogue does not end except when a raid interferes – one from the enemy, and one from the brother. There is no place in the Arab homeland (or "the Arab world") where the shells do not land, targeting the shadow of this woman, whose name I do not know but whom I do know because she is my mother.

—Why are the jets strafing her?

—So that her shadow may disappear from the earth.

—And why does her shadow hurt you so much?

—Because it is heavy. So heavy that the shoulders of this land stretching from the Gulf to the Ocean cannot bear it.

—She asks for nothing more than to be.

—The enemy is not satisfied with that.

—And you? What concerns you more? The satisfaction of the enemy or the life of this woman who is your own blood.

—She is in no position to take on the enemy.

—Do not fight him yourselves. Let her fight him on her own.

—Not from our land. The enemy would not like that.

It has now become possible for the enemy to take a pleasure walk in Arab streets whose occupation he has not yet announced, drinking coffee in cafés or airports, spending the evening in bars, and returning late at night in a taxi or a private car to the borders of Palestine. And if he should get tired of staying up late, he sleeps in our beds. Did he not chase Kamal Nasser, Kamal Adwan, and Mohammad Yousif al-Najjar from their beds?[26]

There was a great display of Arab anger at this insult: millions walked in their funerals. And within one week, Arab jets – defending the safety of the beds of imported ladies – made their own contribution toward the shelling of this woman, whose name I do not know but whom I do know because she is my mother.

—Why are your shells falling on her?

—For her own good. To defend her. We cannot protect her from the raids of the enemy, so we will protect her from a life that brings her nothing but dispersion and us lukewarm reactions from the tourists. It is better for her to die at the hands of her brothers than from the bullets of the enemy.

IV

The cassette opened with the sound of birds singing. It was ten in the morning. The birds do not take a position, and have no interest. Some minutes later the roar of the jets bursts out. (All of a sudden we have become fighters.) Between one attack and another, the birds resume their song.

—Why?

—Because birds don't understand politics.

—Don't they have an instinctive fear of death?

—They do, but they also realize the jets won't hit them on this tree.

—How is that?

—Perhaps they only have fake wings.

—Believe it, or not. I heard them with my own ears, here on this tape.

—What else did you hear?

—That Hong Kong will not be a land of revolution.

—No one is calling for that.

—Where is your body?

—Inside my clothes.

—What are its borders?

—Dates. South: May 15, 1948; East: November 1956; West: June 5, 1967; North: September 1970. These are the borders of my body.

—Are you carrying any grenades?

—No.

—What are you carrying then?

—I'm armed to the hilt with anger.

—Why are you alive?

—To go back to my homeland.

This is the issue. It is not important to bear arms in the street, or the refugee camp, or the home. As long as you bear this body armed to the hilt with anger – as you have just confessed – you are likely to explode and implicate the Arabs. And don't forget that Hong Kong is not the land of revolution. Please allow me to tell you that as long as you are alive, Palestine is alive, and that Palestine cannot be the subject of public discussion because that makes the enemy angry. Angry. Do you understand?

—This is my choice and my destiny. If I'm liberated from choice, I still cannot be released from destiny.

—Go to the [Arab] states that justify their rule and legitimacy by claiming priority in speaking for Palestine. Otherwise, you can do nothing other than become an underwear salesman or work as a doorman in a furnished apartment. Because the enemy will get angry, angry, and our house is made of glass.

—I was born here. I'm not a refugee. I was born here twenty-five years ago. I'm not a refugee. Hong Kong is not the land of revolution. I'm not a refugee. But why should it be Saigon?

—Because the enemy will get angry.

—Where shall I go then?

—Go to the Arab revolution.

—Where is it?

—I don't know.

Then I listened to the rest of the cassette. The roar of the jets and the shells mixed with the sounds of the birds.

V

I paused over this continent, surrounded by the sea and the ocean, and declared: I come from the apex of defeat. This land seems like a wounded bull that fell from the pinnacle of hope to the lowest depths of hereditary defeat and was connected to the world only by a sharp horn that still hovers over the surface of the earth, overflowing with oil, lethargy, and people forbidden any role except filling out ballots whose results always come out YES.

(The king took off his royal robes and put on a military officer's uniform. He seized the radio station and declared a republic. He announced that the government which had been toppled was conspiring to sell out Palestine, but that he had embarked on a glorious revolution for the sake of liberating Palestine and achieving Arab unity. Everyone applauded. They moved from a state of despair to a state of nondespair. The king was laughing in his bedroom, pleased that the poll results had all come out YES.)

You sheathed the horn of the bull in your chest and turned into something between a body and a corpse – a third figure ready for a new name. They gave you a name, and you believed in it, without fully realizing that you were nothing more than an irritant in the nerves of a state of affairs that hovers at the crossroads of choice.

—Your blood versus petrol. That is the core of the struggle.

The regimes needed this equation in order to put pressure on the overseas consumer. They cheered for you, and the color of oil was bolder than your blood when they first met.

Something is ready to erupt, but is prevented from doing so. That is you. All the nationalistic songs are meant for you, as well as tons of tents, and a wall for posters.

A revolutionary caught in the fist of a king. Do you know how to play the game correctly? These masses who grant you their hopes and their bread – the king hides them under his white cloak in your name.

This thing that stretches from the water in the east to the water in the west, what is its name? It is not a map, and it is not a homeland. Yet it is a body waiting for an earthquake to arise from a prophet whose prophecy does not obey any rule except to call things by their names. You are not the alternative, or the savior. But you are the sign, the beginning, and the sacrifice. And things have begun to move.

—Your blood and petrol. This is the struggle that remains after the fall of all previous experiments and slogans.

Why is your blood so radiant that its color is more powerful than the color of oil? The consumer overseas begs you to bring petrol back to its untroubled state in exchange for a promise to return a piece of land. They took steps to bring you back to the fist of the king in a game that you have not mastered. Your role ended, and you are now back to your previous state of being: a refugee with a cause. They said to the people, "This is your internal enemy who is inciting the external enemy against you." They granted safe passage to the common enemy because the equation had now changed: the security of the enemy had become one with the security of the regimes. They gave the enemy breathing space, and set about defending his security and borders, which were now tightening their grip on the necks of their capitals. The defense of the Sublime Port entails defending the sleep and comfort of the conquerors. Students asked anxiously, "What's the difference between conquerors who come from outside and oppressors who emerge from within?" They differed on many points, but they agreed on this, that conquerors bring dispersion and exile while oppressors finish off anyone who survives the grip of the conquerors.

As for you, you are still waiting on a continent surrounded by the sea and the ocean, crying out: "I come from the apex of defeat to protect the bull's horn floating on the surface of the earth, which is my chest."

VI

You are growing older together, you and May.

Your shoulders grow bigger, and so does the rock. May then offers its credentials to the month that follows it, and the state of affairs remains a contest. It should have been hard for May to reach a quarter of a century with such ease, with no change in the quiescent war. Is history not a joker? That – after all these defeats and the entanglements of these months – the war should be raging in our own streets in order to let the enemy finish his celebrations? Is history not a joker? May exits to usher in June, and Arab guns are aiming in all directions except the correct one. If a laborer complains or a student feels rage, our guns do not lack courage. The war is domestic on all fronts, and we sing for steadfastness. A quarter of a century! A quarter of a century and we are still chewing on the same sentence, while the enemy's borders are chasing us. More speeches, and more defeats, and you are the exception to the rule.

—O wandering Palestinian, bring an end to this chaos.

You did not pay heed, so they led you to another massacre in another month, or on the anniversary of your first death. For what? For the sake of an imaginary peace.

You will become a ghost. You will become a nightmare. You will become a spark.

—Go somewhere else and leave us in peace.

—Wherever I go, my shadow becomes a place.

When a stray bullet brings down a horse in the arena, society ladies and lovers of horse races will grieve.

But when the bullets target scores of people in their homes, no one in the city grieves.

There are no names or photos for these victims, because a martyred horse covers the universe.

Why do martyrs fall in such great numbers for nothing, and in places that are not suitable for martyrdom? Death has become a profession for many. What would happen if those who are candidates for death were to declare a strike against this profession? What would happen?

—We will then become a people without martyrs, and the dead will have died in vain.

—What else?

—The poets will go bankrupt.

—Again, what else?

—The orators will start stammering.

—And what else?

—The government will fall.

—Liquidation? We do not think so. This is an internal matter. Our relations are good. For the sake of sovereignty and mutual concern for national independence, we do not interfere. Liquidation? Why use this expression? We call this "independence." The watchword in use at this stage is not the liberation of the occupied Arab land from the Israeli conquerors. The watchword now is the liberation of Arab lands from those who pose a threat to the internal security of the regimes in the Middle East, and from those who keep reminding people that their homeland is occupied. This of course is not liquidation. Who is responsible? It is not one person, or an agency within a regime. It is the official Arab environment. Within the confines of this stagnant environment internal oppression becomes legitimate under the banner of safeguarding national sovereignty. The weight of the Palestinian question is heavier than any shoulder can bear, so why should we bear it alone? This is what they say. In such a general atmosphere any aggression against the revolution – not only the Palestinian – becomes solely an internal matter.

—If you kill them, we will walk in their funerals. But if this cannot be done quickly, we will find ourselves in a dilemma and must interfere for the sake of reconciliation.

Who is responsible then?

The condition of undeclared peace in Arab practice, and the condition of declared war in the Arabic sentence.

Appendix

❧

A State of Waiting: Introduction

Once at Le Bourget Airport in Paris, and again on a street in Sofia, your destiny was calling on you to decide. And your identity – obscure on paper but shining in the heart – demanded concord between them. As if in one stride you had leapt from the beginning of your life to the question, "Who are you?"

The French police could not understand something the Israeli police themselves did not understand. Your travel document declares that your citizenship is obscure. In vain you explain to the French security agent the meaning of this obscurity, since whatever you say calls for yet further grasp of the greater obscurity set into place by his colleague in Tel Aviv. Where were you born? Palestine. Where do you live? Israel. Therefore you are obscure.

In the interrogation room at the airport you contemplate the charge of obscurity and sink into a search for a way to prove your identity. Those who emerged from ancient books have not only taken your homeland, they also took away the means of your belonging to the world. When they were defining their destinies, they were removing from your face the features that would have enabled the world to recognize you. It then became difficult for you to explain the historical distance, which in the understanding of the world has become geographical, between Palestine and Israel. You know you are Palestinian, yet Palestine does not exist in the eyes of the world. And when you try to enter this world you must pass through the vicious tunnel of contradictions: you are a citizen of Israel, but your place of birth, your sense of belonging and your rejection transform you into a complex of ambiguity and contradiction. Therefore, who are you?

Another time in Sofia, what you were facing was not a theoretical question. You were a scandal, a rumor, and a paradox. It is not important now to blame circumstances in order to prove your innocence. All of modern Arab history must stand in the cage of the accused in order for you to accept an accusation from anyone. Before you uselessly answer the judges' question, "What did you do?" you must ask them, "What did you yourselves do that I might have done otherwise?" Once again, this is not really the question, because nonaction on both sides is nothing more than an excuse for prolonging the wrong and worsening the situation.

A few meters away the Palestinian flag with its green, red, white, and black colors was shading a group of young men and women who had come from all corners of their exile. Flying on the horizon the flag was a symbolic recompense for the humiliations of the past, a practical commitment to changing the present, and an epic aspiration for winning the future. How beautiful they were! How beautiful they were! You approached them, carrying within the readiness to be surprised at meeting the half of you that has been lost for twenty years. They were seeking you, also carrying the thirst of twenty years in their souls for the spring now under siege. "We are waiting for you." "We are coming." You cry together, and then part again.

On top of the opposite building to which you were now heading, the Israeli flag with its blue and white colors was shading a group of young men and women of the left. You were not confused between these two feuding flags. The flag of a stolen birthright, and the flag of the crime that possesses a national anthem and a passport. But you were confused in regard to your political action, because it was not enough to know who you were to be saved from the jaws of dilemma. Indeed, you had to know the way to your choice. Have you chosen yet? You came from your occupied homeland holding an Israeli laissez-passer with young people carrying the flag that is your dagger. Where then do you stand?

When at the end of the night the streets of Sofia were empty, you returned to the shadow of your dagger, having left your heart in the nearby building. The ground of perplexity lay between the truth of your being and your current legal status. You have avoided inner battles, but inadequately. You did not go into the hall where the political sessions in this international youth festival were being held, and where the speaker for the Palestinian flag that represents your identity, your truth, and your history clashes with the speaker for the Israeli flag, representing your condition and current situation.

Occasionally, inner harmony would leave you susceptible to error. In the current situation to be in harmony with yourself and your history means to be with your people, for the other choice means to remain where the harmony is disjointed, and having to deal with a state of being that your enemy defines in a way that torments you and that sometimes contradicts your essence. For example, what does it mean for you to be Israeli and Palestinian at the same time? What does it mean to stand in Sofia between two buildings, one flying the Palestinian flag and the other, the Israeli? And are you capable of embodying the Palestinian spirit under the Israeli flag? Or, can you be a thing and its opposite at the same time? And beyond all that, who are you?

.   .   .

The question of identity of the Palestinian Arabs who carry Israeli ID cards has been raised with urgency during the past few years. The issue of this identity is now causing insomnia because the demographic question faced by the Israelis after the occupation of 1967 enters into the picture of what the future of the country, as they imagine it, will be. The presence of nearly a million Arabs with the highest rate of reproduction in the world renders the application of Zionism in the land of Palestine incompatible with what is conceived to be Israel's future in the region. What adds to the urgency of the question are the initial phases of resistance to the Zionist presence that have lately begun to spring up among the Palestinian Arabs whom Israel considers citizens. Add to this the consequence of encountering their brothers in the territories occupied in 1967, which brought about a sense of a shared destiny, and ways of working together. This in turn has led the Israelis to declare disappointedly that the policy of subjugation they had been pursuing toward the Arabs of Israel has failed. Anyone observing the program of "Reassessment" put into place by Israeli officialdom will have noted that Israel was engaged in a two-sided operation. On one hand, to falsify the facts concerning the Arabs living inside Israel by claiming for them an astonishing progress at all levels of life: "No community in the world has progressed and developed in the last twenty-four years at the same rate as the Arab community in Israel," as Shmuel Toledano (the prime minister's adviser on Arab affairs) has declared. This in turn put cheer in the hearts of Israeli cabinet members, who recommended taking advantage "of the current calm to mount a media blitz among the Jewish inhabitants, with multilingual booklets describing Israel's achievements in regard to the Arab minority. The prime minister agreed, but said this was not enough. There must be more action in the media." The other arm of the operation was to search for new ways to suppress the nationalist commitments that come with affiliation to a national community but that are incompatible with their being loyal citizens.

Is it a fact that "no community in the world has developed at the same rate as the Arab community in Israel"? To fall in line with this attempt to reduce the whole issue to a question of development benefits the Israeli authorities, not only because they are the ones who – in possession of the tools of forgery – conduct the census and engineer the figures, but also because this way of framing the issue implies the admission that conquest for the sake of "civilizing" the conquered is the law of interaction between conquerors and conquered peoples. According to this logic, an occupier can gain political, human, and cultural legitimacy because he has been gracious enough to allow occupied peoples to live and breathe. The natural development of people stopped before the arrival of the conqueror. An Arab writer in Israel satirized the practice of the Israeli authorities in ascribing to their actions and good intentions the human development that takes place in the natural course of events: "When Israel was established my daughter was one year old. Now she is twenty. Did she then grow up and reach maturity as a result of Israeli efforts?" This satirical comment brilliantly records the Israeli way of keeping track of human progress. What was the world like before Israel was established, and what is it like now? Before the establishment of Israel, human beings did not land on the moon, and after it was established they landed on the moon three times!

With regard to the question ("Is it true that no community in the world has developed at the same rate as the Arab community in Israel?"), which is only a part of the whole issue, Israel itself cannot hide the exorbitant price that the Arab community has paid, which in fact it was forced to pay, in return for being allowed to live and grow. The Arab fellah who lost his land, which to him was homeland as well as source of livelihood, cannot glorify Israel because under its rule he has been able to earn a loaf of bread only through hard labor in construction, road building, and other menial jobs that Jewish workers find demeaning. It was an Israeli official who expressed the regret that the entire Arab population had not been turned into woodcutters and water sellers. The incomplete realization of such a Zionist dream cannot be attributed to Israeli generosity. Rather it is a victory for the Arab citizen's will to remain steadfast in life, overcoming all obstacles to his development. It is an Israeli failure, not an Israeli bonus.

When Israeli propagandists talk about the "development" of the Arab community in Israel, they are surprised that dissatisfaction and negative response are surfacing among the Arabs, who have rebuffed the Israeli gift of development. As evidence, they repeat that the only possible source of the discontent – that is, martial law – has been removed. But are the Arabs really free from martial law? Nothing has changed except the uniform. After the widespread campaign against the application of martial law to Arab life – its curtailment of the basic freedoms of citizens and its interference in the affairs of their daily life – the government of the previous prime minister was forced to put into effect some easing of this law, which they portrayed as its abolition. What in fact took place was the transfer of authority to enforce the principles of martial law from the army to the police. Yet the legal underpinnings on which martial law is based are still in place, namely, the Emergency Regulations, which remain the foundation for legitimizing oppression and political revenge. These laws are applied only to the Arab citizens. They grant Israeli police the right to detain without trial, to impose travel bans, to enforce house arrest, and to send people into exile. The amazing irony here is that, before Israel came into being, the present leaders of the Israeli establishment described these laws in ways they would now label "anti-Semitic" if used by others. They called them Nazi regulations when they were used against them by the British Mandate. But now these same laws have taken on the mantle of modern human progress for no reason except that the Jews use them against the Arabs. What was Nazi before because it was directed at Jews now becomes progress by the mere fact of its transformation into an instrument of oppression available to these same Jews. On February 7, 1946, the Union of Jewish Lawyers in Palestine severely criticized these Regulations, stating that they "rob citizens of their basic human rights, that they violate the principles of law and justice, that they represent a great threat to the life and freedom of the individual, and that they impose oppression and tyranny without judicial supervision." The matter goes even further. After the establishment of Israel, these laws came under severe attack when they were used against a Jewish religious organization. On June 6, 1951, the Knesset adopted a resolution declaring that the Emergency Regulations "go against the very foundation of a democratic state." It then delegated to a judicial committee the task of abrogating them within two weeks. But these two weeks have not yet ended. These regulations lose their Nazi attributes when used against the Arabs. An Israeli writer has enumerated the advantages of these regulations thus, "They do not allow killing without trial. Other than that, everything is permitted, with no legal repercussions."

These then are the legal bases for oppressing the Arab citizen. When oppression is legalized, its very legality becomes worse than the thing itself, because in this case the oppression would not simply be a question of how a ruler or an authority behaves but the path itself followed by a society and one of the deep-rooted elements of its composition. It was, therefore, on the basis of the legality of this racism that the "Arab community has enjoyed the greatest rate of development in the world," as the Israelis claim.

Does this fabled "development" – and development is in fact an issue for the Arab population in Israel – constitute an alternative to its national cause as a people? And is relative economic development capable of creating an Israeli Arab citizen who would accept absorption into a Zionist body and a commitment to its causes and destiny?

Shmuel Toledano admitted in an interview in the newspaper *Haaretz* that the question of the collective national identity of Israeli Arabs and their absorption into Israeli society and culture is the essence of all the problems faced by the Arab minority. Pinhas Sapir added, "With respect to Arab development in Israel, I have reached the conclusion that, as the quality of life and culture rises, the problems increase and multiply. And I'm afraid that those who believe that improving the quality of life is a substitute for national aspirations have not learned the lessons of history very well. Our experience in Israel tells us that the quality of life, and even more basically, the level of culture, are not particularly effective in holding national aspirations back." Toledano himself also expressed the same idea: "Our experience with Israeli Arabs teaches us that raising the quality of life and culture is not a substitute for national desires and aspirations."

The Israeli print media have recently devoted much space and energy to the analysis of Israeli Arab identity. They were surprised at the failure of

Israel to create the identity it desires for these Arabs. The media observed that nearly sixty thousand Israeli-born Arabs speak Hebrew with total fluency and are part of Israeli life, yet Israeli research into the Arab national question frames the issue solely in terms of Arab disappointment with the Israeli state, which this research ascribes to the Jewish refusal to coexist with them: "The Arabs have to face the phenomenon of widespread fanaticism among the Jewish inhabitants." We also find this: "Fifty thousand Arabs work on Jewish projects in Jewish cities, but Israeli workers are not ready to help them, or befriend them, or consider them partners even in joint professional struggle." And this: "The common tendency among Jews is to maintain the barriers between themselves and the Arab minority." Research undertaken by Dr. Yohanan Peres, lecturer at Tel Aviv University, reached the conclusion that, "The social distance is immense and decisive. The readiness to establish relations with Arabs is extremely low across all social classes and cultural levels. Sephardic Jews are more vehement in their rejection of Arabs than Ashkenazim. 'We know who the Arabs are,' they claim. 'We lived among them and suffered.'" Dr. Peres concludes, "Arab rejection of Jews is less intense than Jewish rejection of Arabs."

In spite of the fact that the Jewish side has the power to express its rejection of the Arab side – a choice not available to the Arabs – this conclusion is extremely valuable because it demonstrates the extent to which racism has penetrated into the organization of Israeli society.

Yet the commentators ignored a significant fact, which is that the refusal of the Jewish people to accept the Arabs does not stem solely from fanaticism but also from the essence of the Zionist idea and its application in Israel. Liberal Israelis have frequently complained that the root cause of the problems stemming from the nonassimilation of the Arabs is the absence of clear guiding principles. This complaint is really nothing more than a misrepresentation of the facts, for Israel's Arab policy has been clear from the establishment of the state: to extirpate them from their lands, to oppress them socially and nationally, to cut them off from their national affiliation, and to create within them a suffocating feeling of severe alienation in their homeland without tempting them with alternatives offers, or compensation. It does not want for them to be Palestinians on one hand, and on the other it cannot and does not want to turn them into Israelis. It therefore decided that keeping them under social and political siege as second-class citizens was the best way to control them, after having failed to expel them all and regretting not having exerted sufficient effort toward that end. Perhaps the policy of violence that culminated in the notorious massacre at Kufr Qasem, which expressed the bitterness of Israeli resentment at the fact that a few Arabs had remained as Oriental decór, served notice to a quarter of a million Arabs that they have only one of two choices, either obedience or death.

The newspaper *Maariv* describes the confusion experienced by the Arabs in Israel in defining their identity thus:

> The dilemma of the Arab is how to be a good Israeli, and how to be a good Arab while remaining a loyal citizen. I asked some Israeli Arabs, "What is your identity?" One of them answered, "I'm a Palestinian citizen of Israel." Another answered, "I'm a citizen of Israel, but my nationality is Arab: an Israeli Arab, just like a Syrian Arab or an Egyptian." A third answered, "I'm an Israeli Arab. Before the establishment of the state, I was a Palestinian Arab."

The paper added that a study of the national identity of Israeli Arabs prepared by two social scientists describes this confusion as "an expert balancing act of inclinations that run counter to each other. A balance that emerges entirely from the lack of a definitive resolution of the question. Israeli Arabs have always lived with the acrobatics of this formula: 'With Israel but not against the Arabs.' Or 'With the Arabs but not against Israel.'" This study analyzed the identity crisis before and after the June War of 1967 as follows:

> With the onset of the tensions that preceded the Six-Day War, the feeling of discomfort among Israeli Arabs was on the rise. The general sentiment was that a resolution of the question of identity was near. A group felt the hour had actually come. Some sent letters of support and some donated money and blood to help the war effort. Yet there were signs of rebellion among others. But the vast majority of the Arab population stayed within the confines of their villages and maintained total silence, as if they had decided that the hour had not yet come to make a decision.

The study adds, "When the war ended, the structure set up to maintain the balance in Israeli Arab identity collapsed, and the humiliation of the Arab world upset the foundations of this sacrosanct hope, which had previously helped to maintain stability. It was difficult to feel confident that the contradiction in the identity was only temporary. An unusual and critical situation had arisen, voices were for advocating a sacred war of liberation, but salvation did not come."

"No other situation resembles that of the Arab minority in Israel," wrote *Maariv*. "Geographically, this minority lives close to the unifying mother nation. Their situation is new: they still remember that only twenty-four years ago they were the majority in the country. They live in a country that is in a state of war with its people. They live within the shadow of the majority's fear that the minority will become the majority." Then Mikhail Assaf offers the following conclusion: "Let us not deceive ourselves. The majority of Arab intellectuals are against the state."

Can the Arab individual maintain this equilibrium: to remain Palestinian and Israeli at once. The facts themselves show, as does the debate among Israelis, that both sides are in a permanent state of contention; that the failure of their mutual assimilation, in particular the assimilation of the Arab citizen into the Israeli civic body, does not stem solely from the non-existence of a "judicious" Israeli policy for dealing with the Arab minority; that the struggle reaches all the way back to the long-lasting conflict between the Palestinian Arab on one side and the Zionist on the other, and that the expression "Israeli Arab" is not a coherent concept as much as it is a formulation that draws its usefulness from geographic considerations. Both sides reject assimilation. The Palestinian rejects the Israeli, and the Israeli rejects the Palestinian. Yet in the present circumstances the ability of the Israeli to turn his rejection into an actuality hinders Arabs living in Israel from settling the question of their identity and therefore their participation in civic life and their self-determination.

The adviser for Arab affairs admitted the impossibility of reconciling the contradiction between the two identities in the following statement: "Almost every day we hear and read that we must build a bridge for dialogue." And, "We must find a common denominator between us and the Arabs." These are beautiful words, but I ask you, Mr. Toledano, what have the government, the state, and the society done to realize this harmony with the Arab inhabitants in our everyday life? To answer the question honestly, Toledano had to cover up all the signs of suppression, discrimination, and subjugation to which the Arabs are subject. "The government has accomplished what it undertook to do," he answered. "All restrictions have been removed, whether in regard to martial law, the closed areas, or land confiscation." "Are these measures enough?" he was asked. And he answered, "No. They are not enough. But this is what the government can do."

Here again the attempt to merge the Arab into the Zionist framework led to an impasse; for, just as the so-called economic development did not curb the national aspirations of the Arabs in Israel or cancel their identity, so the assumption of equality and the opening of whatever doors of opportunity it has been possible to open can never, in the absence of a complete reversal in Israeli policy, resolve the impossible equation of identity. It seems that it is hard for the Israelis to realize that they are occupiers of the Palestinian homeland, and that the Arab minority is a people under occupation. That is the primary truth of interaction between the two peoples. It also seems difficult for them to understand that a quarter century of occupation does not change the fact of occupation or the awareness of the Arab person that he is occupied, nor will it turn him into an Israeli citizen by his own volition. Israeli politicians have exerted much energy to alter this awareness, but to no end. They tried everything to get the Arab psyche to accept the permanence of this situation, in the hope that the Arabs may get used to it and forget about their national identity in their preoccupation with matters of daily life. But shocks and crises have always demonstrated the impossibility of convincing the Arabs that they are Israeli citizens. They never adopted Israeli identity, and they were never given a choice between being Israel citizens or not. The political setup within the country allowed them only one choice, namely, to work within the framework legally allowed by the state as part of the overall Zionist establishment. The condition for working within this establishment is the nonnegotiable acceptance of the Zionist essence. Therefore, the only liberty allowed the Arabs, given the internal and external circumstances of the country for the past quarter century, was that of conditional objection to the forms and dimensions of Zionist practice, and the freedom to call for reforms from within the Zionist establishment. This liberty ends, or turns into "disloyalty" or "spying," if it goes as far as objecting to the Zionist principle itself. Doing so is considered clandestine behavior forbidden by law, and the Arab then finds himself outside the sphere of political action altogether. Therefore, to the extent that the negation of freedom is a form of slavery, the freedom allowed Israeli Arabs resembles slavery because the very basis for practicing this freedom is the acceptance of the justness of Israel's claims.

Why should the Arabs accept an aspect of freedom that is devoid of liberty? Under certain political conditions, this acceptance becomes a destiny, because, failing that, only one of two alternatives remains available. The first would be to forget about working within permissible limits, which would mean forgetting about the homeland for the moment in order to choose the freedom of total and committed objection to a Zionist Israel by joining one of the resistance groups. The other alternative is clandestine resistance inside the occupied country – and that would mean giving up on the potential effectiveness of political action permitted by Israeli law. But this is an alternative that cannot be undertaken solely from the perspective of personal courage and national feelings, without consideration of what can be achieved within the context of the Arab-Israeli conflict.

Israeli Arabs cannot establish independent organizations, and this forces them to engage in political activity by working within Israeli parties. During certain phases in the Arab-Israeli conflict, Arab participation in leftist parties is considered progressive within the existing political balance, especially since priority will be given to issues arising from the most pressing problems of daily life and not to discussion of the Zionist structure of the state. The Arabs in Israel are part of the Palestinian Arab people. It is difficult to affirm this identity inside Israel because such an affirmation entails a commitment to one's destiny and to the battle. It is not easy for the Communist Party (the only party in Israel in which Israeli Arabs engage in political activity) to affirm this identification on a permanent basis, not because the identity is a subjective point of view that can be disputed, but because the party determines the manner in which this national minority can approach their Palestinian brothers.

Now, how does this national minority struggle these days, and what is its political role? Writing in the newspaper *Davar* about the Arabs who used to belong to the national movement known as "The Land" (a movement that attempted to establish an independent Arab political organization), Ehud Yaari says that they are divided into three groups. "There are those who continue with political activity within newly established structures. There are those who have given up on the possibility of struggle inside Israel. And there are those who have reached the conclusion that there is no other choice but terrorism." The writer adds, "Every young person with a national feeling now faces the choices confronting the leaders of 'The Land' movement after their organization was eradicated: to work with the Communist Party (Rakah), to abandon politics altogether, to join the established order, or to resort to terrorism. Each of these choices entails having to give up on priorities or to subject oneself to danger. In all cases the choice is difficult."

There now appears to be a consensus in the Arab community that the alternative to giving up on politics is working with Rakah on the understanding that such a move precludes absorption into the life of the state, or resorting to armed struggle. At the Seventeenth General Meeting of

Rakah the party delineated Arab national identity in the following terms: "The Arab citizens in the state of Israel are a national minority and form part of the Palestinian Arab people." The program specified their struggle and political role thus:

> They are struggling to achieve civic and national equality before the law in the state of Israel, and for social progress and democracy, in order to achieve their national rights and justice for the Palestinian Arab people as a whole. They also strive for a just peace between Israel and the Arab countries. To achieve these aspirations for progress and democracy and bring about a fundamental change in the course of Israeli policy, the Arab citizens wage a joint struggle with democratic Jewish forces against a government policy which serves the interests of imperialism; against the policy of injustice and national oppression; and against reactionary policies that are contrary to the interests of the masses and working people. For these reasons the Arab citizens of Israel constitute an important progressive force in the fight against imperialism.

The Communist Party thereby limits the political struggle of the Arabs in Israel to this democratic framework, as we can also see from the following point in its program: "Before the June War and after, the Arab citizens rejected all attempts to push them into dangerous means of struggle which serve no interest but to bring harm to them and to the general struggle for democracy in Israel."

Israeli Arabs cannot establish their own political organizations on the basis of national identity. "The Arabs of Israel are subject to psychological exhaustion." Thus says Toledano, adding (during the week that a secret organization was discovered) that there are no secret or semisecret Arab organizations. It is truly laughable that Israel should deal with this exhaustion by promoting its Arab agents to high positions. The Zionist frame of mind still insists that appointing an Arab to a high position will compensate the Arab population in Israel for their tragedy. It is also laughable that the Israeli authorities resorted to tempting these people by opening the doors of the ruling Labor Party to them. We have not seen a hangman yet who tries to gain the affection of his victim by giving them a part in the production of the rope. Shimon Peres suggests the formation of an Arab bloc, or a "fraternal Arab party," but it quickly became clear to party leaders that there are no partial solutions here, for a simple reason: if the Arabs are not going to be accepted in the Labor Party, they will form an independent Arab party. Therefore those in the Labor Party who are against opening the door to the Arabs know that any other alternative is less acceptable. The electoral strength of Israeli Arabs is such that they would be able to bring the third largest block into the Knesset after Labor and Gahal – that is, between thirteen and fourteen members. Thus says *Maariv*, adding that "Golda Meir, Pinhas Sapir, and others are not happy about opening the door of their party to the Arabs, but they consider that to be the lesser of two evils." In summary, the ruling party defines the role of the Arabs in politics in these terms: as an occasion for propaganda; as proof of electoral strength; and as an evil that must be drafted into its service in order for them to accept the destiny already decided for them, convincing them that they are part of its political and social life without actually wishing to make them a part or to grant them equality. All this adds up to making them a part of the party's political life through obedience, without actually being part of it in terms of their rights.

In short, Israel has not been able to create the ideal Arab model, or the Israeli Arab citizen as the term is understood. More than that, it has not been able to make a truce with them. Their war is silent, but effective. And their survival – just the fact of being there – and their role in political life, however modest, is a victory in the tough war they have been waging for the past quarter century by all available means: dissent (silent or declared), demonstrations, strikes, procreation, leftist politics, secret action, poetry, identity, insistence on saying, "We are Arab," patience, waiting, attachment to sentimental and nationalist songs heard on Arab radio stations. Are they psychologically exhausted? Yes, but they do not surrender. They speak Hebrew better than any Israeli minister, but the language does not embrace or contain them. That which exhausts them most is the long wait, yet waiting feeds their identity on a daily basis. Their hopes are often disappointed, but disappointment is nothing more than the rejection that they harbor for their situation and an expression of attachment to their nation. They wait because they feel that their condition is temporary. The waiting that exhausts them is also draining the hope of those who usurped their country that they will succeed in forcing the Arabs to surrender and obey. But the Arabs sit in their throats like thorns. They adapt their rejection according to prevailing conditions and available means. They know their identity and they sometimes feel confused, but then their awareness of the identity of their conquerors brings back their previous equilibrium. Sometimes, due to their preoccupation with earning their bread, they forget they are occupied, but they bring children into the world who do not forget. Israeli observers were stunned when they found out that the new generation – the generation born under occupation – feels more strongly the attachment to its national identity and its rejection of the Israeli state.

"The Arabs who live in Israel – their condition does not resemble the condition of any other people in the world." Thus say the Israelis. The state of alienation generated in them by the Israeli occupation has not extended to alienation from their affiliation and identity. They responded to it by alienation from the Israeli condition. True, they live under occupation as strangers in their homeland, but they are not strangers to their homeland. Toledano sees the past quarter century in terms of three phases. The first was the "phase of waiting," which stretched from 1948 to the Sinai War [1956]: "At that time the Arabs of Israel were in a state of waiting. They were not sure about the fate of this state, whether it was going to remain or pass." The second was "the phase of partial acceptance," which stretched from the Sinai War to the Six-Day War: "In this phase the Arabs learned to accept the existence of the state, but there were serious complaints against martial law, the policy of land confiscation, the absence of freedom of movement, and other such matters." The third was the "phase of complete acceptance," which began in 1967 and continues still today: "The state of Israel is a fact, and economic development is proceeding apace. All complaints by the Arabs against the government have now come to an end." He adds: "In this phase difficult questions have arisen which were not there before. They ask themselves, 'Who are we? What is our place in this state? And what does the future hold for us as a national minority in the Jewish state of Israel?'" Toledano knows that it is not possible to offer answers to these difficult questions, and that the loyalty of the Arabs to Israel remains in doubt as long as "there is no peace between Israel and the Arabs."

This admission subsumes another that the Israelis do not want to articulate. Arab acceptance of their own situation, whether partial or total, or outward appearances that encourage this perspective, cannot become real because they can take other, divergent, forms, should external Arab action lead to rekindled hopes. The state of waiting then becomes all they have left. Consider the moral and psychological reactions of these citizens during the War of Attrition, or the rise in acts of resistance. What appears to be acceptance is nothing more than human nature – human beings going about their daily life in ordinary times when there is no other alternative. We would not be exaggerating if we were to say that the phase which Toledano calls "complete acceptance" (the days following the 1967 June War and a little before that) was the very phase that brought back to the consciousness of the Arabs that their situation is provisional. Those days made them acutely aware of the fact of occupation, canceling whatever preliminary acceptance they might have felt. The general feeling was that they were not simply an oppressed minority struggling for democracy and equal rights before the law, but an occupied people standing at the gates of salvation. The reunion of the Israeli Arabs with their other half in the Occupied Territories after the defeat of 1967 deepened their consciousness that they too were under occupation despite the fact that they held Israeli identity cards and spoke Hebrew and were able to adjust to an Israeli lifestyle. The distinctive qualities of the one Palestinian people and their way of life, their destiny, their family relations, and the reawakening of the longing that had fallen asleep due to excessive drowsiness were more powerful than a quarter century of attempts to suppress this distinctiveness. They also realized that the ebb and flow in the manner of giving expression to the condition of waiting that characterized their life in Israel did not signify any confusion in the knowledge of their identity. That identity was starkly clear, but bewilderment stemmed from the confused state of external Arab action – whether this action moved forward or was set back. They realized further that the various methods they use in conducting their struggle were not determined by internal Israeli conditions as much as by the state of the Arab-Israeli conflict.

They wait, and waiting is steadfastness and a stand.

Endnotes

FOREWORD

1. For a discussion of Darwish's use of "the obscure" (first part of the appendix) and a more detailed analysis of the ideas broached here, see my article, "Contexts of Language in Mahmoud Darwish," *Georgetown University Center for Contemporary Arab Studies*, http://ccas.georgetown.edu/79055.html.

THE MOON DID NOT FALL INTO THE WELL

2. The fate of al-Birwa is described in *All That Remains: The Palestinian Villages Occupied and Depopulated by Israel in 1948*, Walid Khalidi, ed. (Beirut: Institute for Palestine Studies, 2006), pp. 9–10. A complete list of the destroyed Palestinian villages is also available online at Palestine Remembered, http://www.palestineremembered.com.

3. Josh. 24:13. (New American Standard Bible).

4. See Alfred M. Lilienthal, *The Zionist Connection II: What Price Peace?* (Brunswick: North American, 1982), p. 151. Lilienthal cites this passage from a 1940 entry in Herzl's diary as a corroborative example in his discussion of the "original [Zionist] plan to uproot and displace the Arab population by any and all means possible." The sentence in brackets is not included in Lilienthal.

5. Not an exact quotation. The expression "The Day of the Lord" occurs more than twenty times in the Hebrew Bible, most often with reference to the end of times when there will be a cataclysm.

6. On the ethnic cleansing of Palestine, see *The Ethnic Cleansing of Palestine* by the prominent Israeli historian Ilan Pappé (Oxford: Oneworld Publications, 2006). On "historical resentment," compare Pappé's assessment: "But the window of opportunity will not stay open forever. Israel may still be doomed to remain a

country full of anger, its actions and behavior dictated by racism and religious fanaticism, the features of its people permanently distorted by the quest for retribution," p. 256.

7. See S. Yizhar, *Khirbet Khizeh* [first published in Hebrew in 1949], trans. Nicholas de Lange and Yaacob Dweck (Jerusalem: Ibis Editions, 2007), pp. 107–8.

8. Translated from Darwish's Arabic text. The complete quotation is as follows: "In the eyes of the younger, post-Zionist generation, the Holocaust has thus come to confirm one of the basic tenets of classical nineteenth-century Zionism: without a country of your own you are the scum of the earth, the inevitable prey of beasts." See Amos Elon, *The Israelis: Founders and Sons* (New York: Holt, Rinehart and Winston, 1973), p. 204.

9. On the use of the Holocaust to nurture a sense of Jewish identity, consider Boas Evron's assessment in *Jewish State or Israeli Nation?* (Bloomington: Indiana University Press, 1995), p. 250: "For many Jews, the Holocaust is now the only meaning and content of Judaism and the very basis of their identity as Jews." In an interview, Tom Segev confirms the equation of Holocaust and identity, "For many, many Israelis, the Holocaust has become a very central element of identity." (Harry Kreisler, Israeli National Identity: Conversation with Tom Segev, http://globetrotter.berkeley.edu/people4/Segev/segev-con0 .html. [Original source: Conversations with History, Institute of International Studies, University of California, Berkeley (April 8, 2004).]

10. On the uses of the Holocaust to foster the notion of Israeli victimhood and extract money from Swiss banks, see Norman G. Finkelstein, *The Holocaust Industry: Reflections on the Exploitation of Jewish Suffering* (London: Verso, 2000). On the manipulation of the Holocaust for purposes of the Israeli state, see Tom Segev, *The Seventh Million: The Israelis and the Holocaust* (New York: Hill and Wang, 1993). Boas Evron (cited by Darwish later in the text) objects to the very term "the Holocaust" and the way it has been used by successive Israeli governments to justify expansionist aims and to suppress criticism: "Two awful things happened to the Jewish people in the present [twentieth] century: the Holocaust – and the lessons drawn from it." See "Holocaust: The Uses of Disaster," *Radical America* 17.4 (1983): 7–21; this article is also available online. In this connection, see also Gideon Levy, "Holocaust remembrance is a boon for

Israeli propaganda," *Haaretz*, http://www.haaretz.com/hasen/spages/1145670 .html (January 4, 2010).

11. The reference here is to Bertolt Brecht's *The Caucasian Chalk Circle*.

12. I am unable to confirm the accuracy of the "citation" from Buber. However, in "Two Peoples in Palestine," a talk given on Dutch radio in 1947 (and in other places in his writings as well), Buber's view of Jewish exceptionalism confirms Darwish's conclusions concerning the perceived Jewish "I-Thou" relationship to the land of Palestine: "You must set before you," Buber says, "that the Jews are not a people like all others . . . They are a unique phenomenon, unlike any other: a society in which peoplehood, on the one hand, and faith, on the other, have been melted down together and refined into a unity that cannot be sundered. And that faith has been bound up from its beginning with this land." See "Two Peoples in Palestine," in Paul Mendes-Flohr, ed., *A Land of Two Peoples: Martin Buber on Jews and Arabs* (Chicago: University of Chicago Press, 2005), pp. 195–96. It is doubtful that Buber advocated population transfer. As the title of his talk makes clear, he advocated a "binational" state in Palestine. For a trenchant critique of the ahistorical blending of religion (God), ethnos (Chosen People), and the Land of Palestine, see Shlomo Sand, *The Invention of the Jewish People*, trans. Yael Lotan (New York: Verso, 2009). For an equally trenchant critique of the archaeology of Palestine based on a biblical perspective, see Keith W. Whitelam, *The Invention of Ancient Israel: The Silencing of Palestinian History* (New York: Routledge, 1996).

13. See *Three Days and a Child* by A. B. Yehoshua, trans. by Miriam Arad (London: Peter Owen, 1970), pp. 131–74. The relevant passages in Arad's translation of "Facing the Forests" are: the Arab's tongue, p. 140; names of donors, p. 147; procession of Crusaders, p. 151; location and map of village, p. 153; animal-like sounds, pp. 165–66; abstract drawing, p. 170.

14. See Elon, p. 271.

JOURNAL OF AN ORDINARY GRIEF

15. I have chosen to translate Darwish's somewhat abridged text directly, rather than reproduce the entire dialogue verbatim as it occurs in Elon, p. 182.

16. The novel in question is most likely Nikos Kazantzakis's *Captain Michalis* (1953), which appeared in translation in many of the world's languages, including Hebrew, as *Freedom or Death*.

17. *The Arabs in Israel* by Sabri Jiryis. First Arabic edition published by the Institute for Palestine Studies in Beirut in 1973. Jiryis, a lawyer, consulted the court records that Darwish cites. English translation by Inea Bushnaq (New York: Monthly Review Press, 1977).

18. The citation from Ahad Ha'am is translated from Darwish's Arabic text. Compare the following translation from the Hebrew by Hilla Dayan: "And what do our brothers do? Exactly the opposite! They were slaves in their diasporas, and suddenly they find themselves with unlimited freedom, wild freedom that only a country like Turkey can offer. This sudden change has planted despotic tendencies in their hearts, as always happens to former slaves [*'eved ki yimlokh*]. They deal with the Arabs with hostility and cruelty, trespass unjustly, beat them shamefully for no sufficient reason, and even boast about their actions. There is no one to stop the flood and put an end to this despicable and dangerous tendency." Excerpt from Ha'am's "A Truth from Eretz Yisrael," in *Wrestling with Zion: Progressive Jewish-American Responses to the Israeli-Palestinian Conflict*, ed. Tony Kushner and Alisa Solomon (New York: Grove Press, 2003), p. 15. See also Tom Segev, *One Palestine Complete: Jews and Arabs under the British Mandate*, trans. Haim Watzman (New York: Henry Holt, 1999), p. 104. The quotation from *Wrestling with Zion* is available online at http://www.groveatlantic.com/grove/bin/wc.dll?groveproc~genauth~3111~4164~excerpt.

19. Kufr Qasem was not the only massacre carried out in 1956. Two other massacres of Palestinians were committed by the Israeli army in the Gaza Strip, which Joe Sacco reconstructs from oral history and illustrates with vivid cartoons in his graphic novel *Footnotes in Gaza* (New York: Henry Holt, 2009). "According to figures from the United Nations," notes Patrick Cockburn in his review of this book in the *New York Times*, "275 Palestinians were killed in the town of Khan Younis at the southern end of the strip on Nov. 3, and 111 died in Rafah, a few miles away on the Egyptian border, during a Nov. 12 operation by Israeli troops," *The New York Times Book Review*, December 24, 2009. A Google book search will yield a number of studies of Israeli massacres.

20. Ze'ev Jabotinsky's words are cited from Colin Shindler, *The Triumph of Military Zionism: Nationalism and the Origins of the Israeli Right* (London: I. B. Tauris, 2006), p. 94.

21. Actually, at least one of them, the historian Shlomo Sand, did come back. See the description of his friendship with Darwish and those drinking sessions in *The Invention of the Jewish People*, pp. 7–9. Sand reveals here that Darwish's famous 1967 poem "A Soldier Dreams of White Lilies" was written for him.

IMPROVISATIONS ON THE SURA OF JERUSALEM

22. There is no Jerusalem sura in the Qur'an. Before Mecca, Jerusalem was the first *qibla* (direction one faces in prayer) for Muslims. The "Farther Mosque" in the opening verse of Sura 17, "The Night Journey," is understood by Muslim tradition to be a reference to Jerusalem: "Praise Him who brought his servant by night from the Holy Mosque to the Farther [Aqsa] Mosque . . ." [my translation].

23. Darwish here is citing the opening words of the chant sung during the Good Friday matins (service held on Thursday night) in the community of churches that practice the Byzantine rites: "Today was hung upon the Cross [literally, "a piece of wood"]. He who hung the earth upon the waters."

24. This passage echoes Christ's words in Luke 23:28, as he was being led to the scene of the Crucifixion: "Daughters of Jerusalem, do not weep for me; no, weep for yourselves and your children" (*The New English Bible*, Oxford University Press, 1971), p. 4.

25. "Jerusalem the Golden" (usually translated as "Jerusalem of Gold") is the name of a song that was popular in Israel in the lead-up to the June War of 1967, and became extremely popular after the war as a triumphalist celebration of the conquest of East Jerusalem.

GOING TO THE ARABIC SENTENCE ON MAY 15

26. These three PLO leaders were assassinated (along with al-Najjar's wife) in Beirut on April 10, 1973, in an Israeli operation reputedly led by Ehud Barak dressed as a woman. Kamal Nasser was a noted Palestinian poet.